D0506408

Joomla! Social Networking with JomSocial

Enhance your social networking with JomSocial

Learn how to develop a high quality social network with JomSocial

Beatrice A. Boateng

Kwasi Boateng

[PACKT] open source ✳

PUBLISHING

community experience distilled

BIRMINGHAM - MUMBAI

Joomla! Social Networking with JomSocial

Copyright © 2010 Packt Publishing

All rights reserved. No part of this book may be reproduced, stored in a retrieval system, or transmitted in any form or by any means, without the prior written permission of the publisher, except in the case of brief quotations embedded in critical articles or reviews.

Every effort has been made in the preparation of this book to ensure the accuracy of the information presented. However, the information contained in this book is sold without warranty, either express or implied. Neither the authors nor Packt Publishing and its dealers and distributors will be held liable for any damages caused or alleged to be caused directly or indirectly by this book.

Packt Publishing has endeavored to provide trademark information about all of the companies and products mentioned in this book by the appropriate use of capitals. However, Packt Publishing cannot guarantee the accuracy of this information.

First published: July 2010

Production Reference: 1120710

Published by Packt Publishing Ltd.
32 Lincoln Road
Olton
Birmingham, B27 6PA, UK.

ISBN 978-1-847199-56-0

www.packtpub.com

Cover Image by Asher Wishkerman (a.wishkerman@mpic.de)

Credits

Authors
Beatrice A. Boateng
Kwasi Boateng

Reviewer
Jose Argudo Blanco

Acquisition Editor
Douglas Paterson

Development Editor
Eleanor Duffy

Technical Editors
Mohd. Sahil
Ajay Shanker

Copy Editor
Lakshmi Menon

Indexer
Hemangini Bari

Editorial Team Leader
Akshara Aware

Project Team Leader
Lata Basantani

Project Coordinator
Poorvi Nair

Proofreader
Dirk Manuel

Production Coordinator
Shantanu Zagade

Cover Work
Shantanu Zagade

About the Authors

Beatrice A. **Boateng** is an Assistant Professor in the department of pediatrics, College of Medicine at the University of Arkansas for Medical Sciences. She is also the co-director of faculty development in the department of pediatrics. She holds a doctorate from the Instructional Technology program, College of Education at Ohio University. Beatrice's research interest is in the millennials, instructional technology in medical education and open source tools for education. She has authored articles, book chapters, and a book, on technology applications in rural schools.

A special thanks to Kwasi Boateng for his support throughout the writing of this book.

Kwasi Boateng is an Assistant Professor at the School of Mass Communication at the University of Arkansas at Little Rock. He has a doctorate from The School of Media Arts and Studies (formerly the School of Telecommunications); Scripps College of Communication, Ohio University. Kwasi has research interest in new technologies in electronic communication and open source tools for online communication. He has authored various articles, book chapters, and a book on electronic media. He teaches courses on web design, motion graphics, media and culture, and the Internet regulation and policy. He has worked with students to build websites for non-profit organizations by using open source content management systems, and organizes workshops to introduce high and middle school students to open source tools for online communication.

I am appreciative of the support of Beatrice Boateng, my spouse and co-author of this book. Beatrice has been very instrumental in the writing of this book with her probing questions and her knack for getting things done.

We are grateful to Azrul, the creators of JomSocial who promptly provided us with a copy of the JomSocial component and offered to give us any support that we needed. We also thank the creator of JReviews who similarly offered us a copy of the reviews component. Even though we did not use the product, we note that JReviews is one of the best reviews components for the Joomla! content management system. We also thank the Packt editorial team, who kept us on schedule and made sure that this book was finished on time.

About the Reviewer

Jose Argudo is a web developer from Valencia, Spain. After finishing his studies he started working for a web design company. Then, six years later, he decided to start working as a freelancer.

Now that some years have passed as a freelancer, he thinks it's the best decision he has ever taken—a decision that let him work with the tools he likes, such as Joomla!, Codeigniter, CakePHP, jQuery, and other known open source technologies.

His desire to learn and share his knowledge has led him to be a regular reviewer of books from Packt, such as *Joomla! with Flash, Joomla! 1.5 SEO, Magento 1.3 Theme Design*, and *Symfony 1.3 Web Application Development*.

Recently, he has even published his own book, *Codeigniter 1.7*, which you can also find through Packt's site. If you work with PHP, then take a look at it!

If you want to know more about Jose, you can check his site: `http://www.joseargudo.com`

To my girlfriend and to my brother, I wish them the best.

Table of Contents

Preface

Social networks are ubiquitous. This book is a hand-holding guide to setting up a social network using the Joomla! application. It walks the reader through the process of setting up a social network using Joomla! extensions such as JomSocial, and alternatives such as Community Builder and the jSocialSuite. Also, it illustrates how to integrate other social networks, such as Facebook and Twitter, into a Joomla!-driven social network.

What this book covers

Chapter 1, Not Another Social Networking Site gives an overview of social networks, and introduces us to JomSocial, a Joomla! social networking extension. It walks us through a quick installation of Joomla! as the first step for installing JomSocial.

Chapter 2, JomSocial: Setup and Configuration guides the reader through the following tasks: changing the Joomla! template in preparation for the installation of the JomSocial component; the installation of the JomSocial component, and associated modules and plugins; and determining the initial front-end layout and features of our social networking system.

Chapter 3, Remote Installation and Managing User Profiles takes us through the process of migrating our site from a local machine to a remote server using the Akeeba Backup system. We then start the customization of our social network by setting our default user profiles and privacy features.

Chapter 4, Making Connections with Users and Friends explains how to start making connections within our social network by creating test users, and making connections with other users within the network. It outlines how the messaging system functions as a tool for making connections.

Chapter 5, Creating Content and Sharing Activities illustrates how to create content for our site in order to attract users. It details us how to extend our social network to include a listing and rating system, and how to add features to user profiles. Also, it portrays how to facilitate the sharing of multimedia content.

Chapter 6, Community Building and Interaction documents how to build and manage groups or communities and customize community assets. For instance, it provides information on how to change community avatar, create group content, attract community members, and moderate communities.

Chapter 7, Customizing the JomSocial Template demonstrates how to customize the JomSocial template by duplicating the default template and changing some of its elements.

Chapter 8, Tips and Tricks discusses various tricks that can be used to simplify the user interface. It identifies some code hacks that can be used to make our site adaptable to user needs. For instance, we will make some changes to the JomSocial user profile positions, and integrate JomSocial (our site) with Facebook and Twitter. Also, we address issues related to Joomla! SEF (Search Engine Friendly) links, and modify our site's PHP.ini file.

Chapter 9, Other Joomla! Social Networking Extensions discusses various Joomla! Social networking extensions. For instance, Community Builder, JSocial Suite, Linksutra, CBE, Tuiyo, and Odude. These extensions are to be considered as options available to every Joomla! developer interested in setting up a Joomla!-driven social network.

What you need for this book

The following are the software tools and Joomla! extentions used in this book:

Software:

- A web authoring tool, such as Dreamweaver, Kompozer, or Nvu
- Image editing software, such as Photoshop, Fireworks, or The Gimp
- A text editor

Joomla Extensions:

- JomSocial Component Pro version
- JReviews Component
- Jlord Generator
- Akeebabackup
- JCE Editor

- Kickstart (Akeeba)
- Roketheme Quasar Template

Who this book is for

This book is for individuals or institutions desiring to develop a social network system by using the Joomla! content management system. This book can be used by the novice or the advanced Joomla! user. There is no need for scripting or programming knowledge. All that is required is enthusiasm, and the determination to implement a project.

Conventions

In this book, you will find a number of styles of text that distinguish between different kinds of information. Here are some examples of these styles, and an explanation of their meaning.

Code words in text are shown as follows: "We can include other contexts through the use of the `include` directive."

A block of code is set as follows:

```
<div style="overflow: hidden; visibility: hidden;" onmouseout="joms.
toolbar.closetime()" onmouseover="joms.toolbar.cancelclosetime()"
id="m5">
```

New terms and **important words** are shown in bold. Words that you see on the screen, in menus or dialog boxes for example, appear in the text like this: "Clicking the **Next** button moves you to the next screen".

 Warnings or important notes appear in a box like this.

 Tips and tricks appear like this.

Reader feedback

Feedback from our readers is always welcome. Let us know what you think about this book—what you liked or may have disliked. Reader feedback is important for us in order to develop titles that you really get the most out of.

To send us general feedback, simply send an e-mail to feedback@packtpub.com, and mention the book title in the subject of your message.

If there is a book that you need and would like to see us publish, please send us a note via the **SUGGEST A TITLE** form on www.packtpub.com or send an e-mail to suggest@packtpub.com.

If there is a topic that you have expertise in and you are interested in either writing or contributing to a book on, see our author guide on www.packtpub.com/authors.

Customer support

Now that you are the proud owner of a Packt book, we have a number of things to help you to get the most from your purchase.

Errata

Although we have taken every care to ensure the accuracy of our content, mistakes do happen. If you find a mistake in one of our books—maybe a mistake in the text or the code—we would be grateful if you would report this to us. By doing so, you can save other readers from frustration, and help us to improve subsequent versions of this book. If you find any errata, please report them by visiting http://www.packtpub.com/support, selecting your book, clicking on the **let us know** link, and entering the details of your errata. Once your errata are verified, your submission will be accepted, and the errata will be uploaded to our website, or added to any list of existing errata, under the Errata section of that title. Any existing errata can be viewed by selecting your title from http://www.packtpub.com/support.

Piracy

Piracy of copyright material on the Internet is an ongoing problem across all media. At Packt, we take the protection of our copyright and licenses very seriously. If you come across any illegal copies of our works, in any form, on the Internet, please provide us with the location address or website name immediately so that we can pursue a remedy.

Please contact us at `copyright@packtpub.com` with a link to the suspected pirated material.

We appreciate your help in protecting our authors, and our ability to bring you valuable content.

Questions

You can contact us at `questions@packtpub.com` if you are having a problem with any aspect of the book, and we will do our best to address it.

1
Not Another Social Networking Site

This chapter introduces us to JomSocial, a Joomla! social networking extension. It covers the following:

- An overview of social networks
- Why you may want to create your own social network
- Social networking principles
- Building social networks with JomSocial
- An overview of the JomSocial component of Joomla!
- And a quick installation of Joomla!

Overview of social networking

Just when you think online social networks are old fads, think again. In 2009, the United States' **Defense Advanced Research Projects Agency (DARPA)** launched a network challenge to celebrate the 40th anniversary of ARPANET, the precursor of the Internet. On the morning of December 5, 2009, DARPA launched ten, eight-foot red weather balloons across the United States. The idea was to determine how information goes viral and moves through social networks, and how people can organize themselves through online networks. The task was for people to use online networks to find all ten weather balloons. There was a $40,000 price tag for the winner. With over 4,000 registered teams, the race was on.

The Massachusetts Institute of Technology (MIT) research team used an incentive-based social network model to encourage people to report on their balloon sightings, and within nine hours, all ten balloons were located. With some help from the Facebook and Twitter networks, and with a lot of money at stake, social networks won the day!

This event showcased the power of social networking sites and communities. It proved how effective and efficient online social networks can be. Over the last seven years, we have seen the emergence of online social networks in the form of MySpace, Facebook, Ning, and Twitter to mention just the notable ones.

MySpace (`http://www.myspace.com`) was established in 2003 and purchased by News Corp in 2005, and Facebook (`http://www.facebook.com`), on the other hand, was founded in 2004. Both Facebook and MySpace were developed to primarily facilitate information sharing through social networks. Ning (`http://www.ning.com`), set up in 2005, facilitates the creation of groups or communities within social networks. By 2006, the social networking cyberscape had evolved with the establishment of Twitter, a social networking tool for sharing information in snippets.

There is a growing interest among individuals, businesses, organizations, and communication experts in learning how to set up web-based networks. Joomla! and the JomSocial extension provide cost-effective software solutions for those interested in setting up their own social networking site for whatever reason: business, fun, or venturing into the world of online business startups.

Why create your own social network?

Wouldn't it be fulfilling to know how to build your own social networking site? Since its inception, the Internet has opened up new opportunities for setting up alternate forms of communication. Sites integrated with social networking applications are more dynamic because social networks provide some intrinsic value for the following reasons:

- Internet users are increasingly becoming platform-agnostic (*"Introduction to Mass Communication: Media Literacy and Culture"*, Baran, S. J. (2009), *McGraw-Hill Education*); we do not have preferences for where we access our media content, and social networking sites are proving to be versatile in providing all kinds of media content.
- Social networking sites provide users with the ability to personalize the content of their accounts.
- Social networking sites allow individuals and businesses to connect directly to friends and customers or audiences.
- Social networks differ from regular websites in three fundamental ways:
  - Activities and content are mostly driven by users.
  - Users are expected to do things on the website—interact and post content.

° Users are expected to return periodically to interact with the website. For details, refer to *Applications of usability principles on a social network (2009), Verne Hoe*: `http://creativebriefing.com/applications-of-usability-principles-on-a-social-network`.

Facebook, Twitter, and MySpace are the most popular of such social networks that are used to cater to the needs of individuals, businesses, and organizations. However, the need to integrate social networking into personal, corporate, and organizational websites independent of mammoth social networking sites, such as Facebook, Twitter, and MySpace, make Joomla! and JomSocial invaluable. Also, knowing how to set up such sites provides the opportunity for individuals and organizations to explore innovative ways of communicating.

Principles for setting up a social networking site

A social networking site should provide a mechanism for identity authentication. It should have safety and privacy tools for all users. For more details, please refer to *Joint Statement on Key Principles of Social Networking Sites Safety*: `http://www.state.tn.us/attorneygeneral/cases/facebook/facebookstatement.pdf`.

Social networks are complex systems that need to:

- Engage the user quickly—the immediate user experience is essential. The user interface has to be simple and not distracting, allowing users to add content and change user preference settings.

- Generate new content through the implementation of dynamic applications. This fosters change and interactivity.

- User profile section needs to be customizable to reflect a user's persona. More details can be found at "*3 Principles of Social Network Design*", *David Skul (2007)*: `http://www.buzzle.com/articles/3-principles-of-social-network-design.html`.

A JomSocial social networking site will allow us to do all of these things, and enable us to set up independent social networking sites. And where necessary, JomSocial allows a developer to seamlessly integrate content originating from other mega social networking sites such as Facebook and Twitter into our JomSocial site.

An overview of JomSocial

JomSocial was launched in 2007 by Slashes and Dots Sdn. Bhd., a company based in Malaysia. The company started by developing applications for PalmOS. After one of its products won the Palmsource Enterprise/Productivity Award in 2004, the company began developing components for the Joomla! content management system. The Slashes and Dots are also the developers of NiceTalk, MyBlog, JomWiki, and JomComment.

JomSocial is a commercial Joomla! extension. According to the license agreement, modification of the source code by developers is allowed. However, any form of distribution requires permission from Slashes and Dots (`http://www.jomsocial.com/company/license-agreement.html`).

JomSocial can be purchased through the website (`http://www.jomsocial.com`). The standard version, which comes with a link back to JomSocial, is $99, and the professional version, without the JomSocial link, is $149. You can also obtain a trial version for $1 for 30 days, and pay for a full version after the trial period. The product features vary based on the type of license purchased. You may visit the JomSocial website for updated fee and license agreement information.

Building social networks with JomSocial

After a few years of development, JomSocial has become one of the leading Joomla! social networking extensions. In May 2010, JomSocial was recognized and honored as the best Joomla! application at the 2010 CMS Expo. It is a fully-customizable component, with the ability to:

- Create and manage your own profile
- Add applications to your profile
- Integrate with other third-party components
- Establish a friend system and send private e-mails to friends, invite friends to join the network, and connect with others within the network
- Set up privacy settings for your entire profile and/or applications
- Integrate other notable social networking sites like Facebook, and connect to Twitter and pull tweets from your Twitter account into your JomSocial profile
- Create photo albums and video archives—users can also make comments about your media
- Tag photos in your album
- Archive member activities

Through the use of integrated third-party applications for Joomla!, JomSocial can be extended to include:

- Twitter feeds
- Blogs
- Event listing
- Forum posts
- Google ads

Another great JomSocial feature is the ability to create groups.

- Groups can have their own pages
- The owner of the group can set the membership access level (private or public)
- Group bulletins can be created
- Users can subscribe to group activity streams

JomSocial provides all of the features necessary to create a social network around vibrant communities.

Social Networks on JomSocial

JomSocial has been adopted by several Joomla!-driven websites. It has become the preferred social networking extension for Joomla!. The newly-designed **LINUX.COM** uses it for its Linux community, as shown below:

The **gibLink** website (`http://www.gibLink.com`) is a social networking and marketing site that uses JomSocial for business connections and product promotions. A sample of the gibLlink website can be seen below:

http://www.onlineradiostations.com is a radio station aggregator. This website allows users to share their favorite radio stations and other interesting facts about themselves. A sample screenshot from this website is shown below:

`http://www.backtonormandy.org` is a website dedicated to D-Day. Users can share their stories, pictures, audio clips, and videos about their memories of Normandy. Click on **the PEOPLE** link from the website's home page, to see JomSocial, as shown in the following screenshot.

Let's get started: Joomla! Installation

Throughout this book, we will build a social networking site for mobile phone applications. We will first build the site locally, and then migrate it to a remote host at `http://www.kifari.com`. If you already have a Joomla! 1.5.x-driven website, you can use the steps in the subsequent chapters to extend your site by using JomSocial.

The requirements for installing Joomla! on a localhost and on a remote server of a hosting company are similar. The minimum requirements needed for Joomla! and JomSocial to work are:

- MySQL 4.1 or above
- Apache 1.3 (with mod_mysql, mod_xml, and mod_zlib)
- PHP 5 with:
  - GD library (at least v1.8 with libjpeg)
  - Curl library
  - fsockopen
  - exec
  - FFMPEG
- We recommend that you allocate at least 64 MB of memory to PHP

For remote hosting, you need to ensure that the server environment meets the minimum requirements for installation.

Let's set up the localhost development environment.

Setting up the localhost

To create a development environment that meets the minimum installation requirements, we will use XAMPP. Other alternatives are EasyPhP and WAMP. XAMPP is a free and cross platform software package containing the Apache web server, MySQL database and Perl programming language (`http://www.facebook.com/pages/XAMPP/246915152877`).

1. Go to `http://www.apachefriends.org/en/index.html`.
2. Click on **XAMPP** in the menu.
3. Scroll down and click on **XAMPP for Windows**. We will download xampp-win32-1.7.3.exe (the latest version, at the time of writing).

 You may have to download the appropriate version of XAMPP for your computer's operating system (Mac or Linux).

4. Save the file to your desktop.

Installing XAMPP

Before you can install the software on your computer, you will need to have administrative privileges. Follow these steps:

1. The XAMPP download looks like the icon shown in the following image. Click on the icon to install XAMPP.

2. Click on **Run**.

3. Click on **Install**. XAMPP will create a folder on your C drive. This process takes a few minutes.

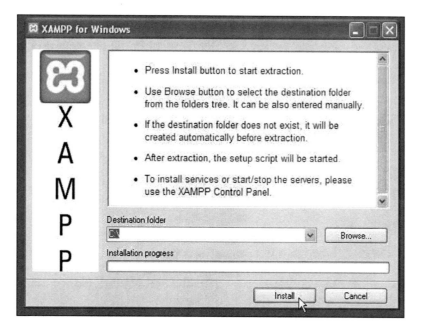

4. After the files are extracted, the XAMPP installation wizard will open a command window with the following messages:

    ○   **Should I add shortcuts to the startmenu/desktop? (y/n)**: Type **y** and press the *Enter* key on your keyboard.

    ○   **Should I locate the XAMPP paths correctly? Should I proceed? (y/x=exit setup)**: Type y and press the *Enter* key on your keyboard.

    ○   **Should I make a portable XAMPP without drive letters? NOTE: you should use drive letters, if you want to use services. With USB sticks, you must not use drive letters. Your choice (y/n)**: Enter **n** and then press the *Enter* key on your keyboard.

    ○   Allow the system to run. When done, press *Enter*.

    ○   The default zone is displayed. We can always change the settings after setup.

    ○   The final message will provide us with other options to edit. Enter **x** and then press *Enter* to close the command window.

Keep the default selections and press the *Enter* key on your keyboard throughout the process.

XAMPP is installed. You will see an **XAMPP Control Panel** shortcut on the desktop. Click on the shortcut to open the XAMPP Control Panel.

 If there is no shortcut on your desktop, go through your Programs menu to find XAMPP. Click on it to activate it.

When the **XAMPP Control Panel Application** opens:

- Click on the **Start** buttons next to **Apache** and **MySql**. Notice the highlighted text **Running** when you click on the buttons.

```
XAMPP Control Panel Application                    _ □ X

[icon]         XAMPP Control Panel                  Shell
               (Apache Friends Edition)             Setup

Modules                                           Port-Check
□ Svc   Apache    Running   Stop    Admin          Explore
□ Svc   MySql     Running   Stop    Admin          SCM
□ Svc   FileZilla            Start   Admin          Refresh
□ Svc   Mercury             Start   Admin          Help
□ Svc   Tomcat              Start   Admin          Exit

XAMPP for Windows Version 1.7.3
Windows 5.1 Build 2600 Platform 2 Service Pack 3
Current Directory: C:\xampp
Status Check OK
Busy...
Apache started
Busy...
MySQL started
```

Let's review what we just did.

We have just installed a development server on our computer. Go to your C drive and you will see the xampp folder. Click on the folder to see all of the files that have been installed on your machine.

Downloading Joomla!

1. To download and save the latest full package version (1.5.x), go to the Joomla! website (`http://www.joomla.org/`) and click on **Download Joomla! Open source content management system**.

2. Create a folder in `c:\xampp\htdocs` and name it `joomla`. Extract the Joomla! files to that folder. The `htdocs` folder is the equivalent of a www root folder, or a `public_html` folder on a remote server provided by a hosting company. The Joomla! files can be seen at: `c:\xampp\htdocs\joomla`.

 You can either use the default file extractor on your computer to extract the files, or use an open source alternative, such as 7-Zip (`http://www.7-zip.org/`).

Installing Joomla! on localhost

To install Joomla! locally, we need a database. Do the following to create the database locally:

1. Go to the **XAMPP Control Panel**. Click on the **Admin** button of **MySQL**. When the browser opens, type in a database name and click on **Create**, as illustrated in the following screenshot. In this example, our database name is **joomla15**.

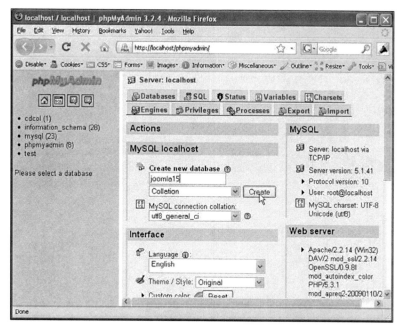

2. Close the window after the database has been created.

3. Open a browser and go to `http://localhost/joomla/` and press *Enter*. This will take us to the **Joomla! Installation** wizard, at the following address: `http://localhost/joomla/installation/index.php`.

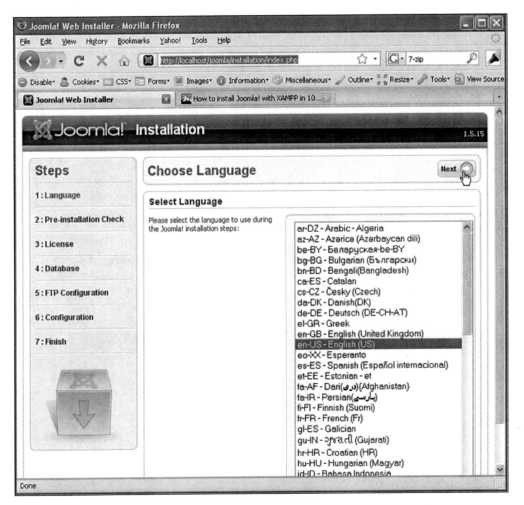

4. Go through the installation process. Under database configuration, enter the settings as shown in the following screenshot.

5. Leave the default settings for FTP, as this is just a local installation.

6. Enter the **Site Name**, **Your E-mail**, and **Admin Password** values, and select **Install Sample Data**.

7. Go to `c:\xampp\htdocs\joomla` and delete the installation folder. We are ready to preview our installation locally. Point your browser to `http://localhost/joomla/`. Congratulations, you just installed Joomla!.

Summary

This chapter explored the importance of social networks, and why we may want to create one. We introduced JomSocial, a Joomla! extension for creating social networks. We wrapped up the chapter by creating a development environment on our computer and then installing Joomla!.

All aboard! Let's build a social networking site!

2
JomSocial: Setup and Configuration

In the last chapter, we gained an insightful background of social networking as a communication phenomenon. We also learned how to install Joomla! locally on a computer. Our next step is to plan our social network. Our goal is to develop a website for reviewing cell phone apps. Users of our site will be able to list, review, rate, and recommend cell phone apps. Also, they will be able to upload informational and instructional multimedia content about apps.

In order to build our apps review site, we will install and configure the JomSocial component, and related modules and plugins.

In this chapter, we will perform the following tasks:

- Change our Joomla! template
- Install the JomSocial component, and associated modules and plugins
- Configure JomSocial through the component's administrator back-end
- Create a link to the social network (JomSocial) within Joomla!
- Determine the front-end layout and features of the social networking system

Changing the Joomla! template

Our current site on the development server is a basic installation of Joomla! populated with sample content. We will begin by removing the sample content from our site. Please refer to *"Joomla! 1.5: Beginner's guide"*, *Eric Tiggeler*, *Packt Publishing* for information on how to disable front-page content. If we already have content on our site, we may want to rearrange it as we develop our social network.

Now let's concentrate on changing the look and feel of our site by adopting another Joomla! template. We will use the GPL (General Public License) Quasar template from RocketTheme (http://www.rockettheme.com). We chose a RocketTheme template because their team is one of the most innovative Joomla! theme developers, and one of their templates, Affinity, won Packt's Best Joomla! Theme Award in 2009 (http://www.packtpub.com/joomla-award).

To access the Quasar template:

1. Go to: http://www.rockettheme.com/.

2. Click on **Joomla! | Joomla Templates**. The Quasar template can be found under **Joomla Free Templates** and was released in January 2010.

3. Download the Quasar template file: rt_quasar_j15.tgz.

To install the template:

1. Log in to the Joomla! administrative back-end.

2. Go to: http://localhost/joomla/administrator. Log in with the appropriate username and password.

3. Click on **Extensions** on the top menu, and then choose **Install/Uninstall** from the drop-down menu.

4. Once the **Extensions Manager** has opened, under the **Install** option, click on **Upload Package File**, and then click on **Browse**. Locate the rt_quasar_j15.tgz file, select it, and then click on **Open**.

5. Click on **Upload File & Install**. We will see the **Install Template Success** message if our template installation was successful.

6. Make this the default template by going to **Extensions | Template Manager**. Select the template and set it as the default.

7. Refresh the website to view the changes.

A new template may change the layout of the site. And, if we have content, we may want to rearrange it. The Quasar template modification instructions can be found on the RocketTheme website.

> For comprehensive discussions on how to modify Joomla! and Joomla! templates, refer to *"Joomla! 1.5 Beginner's guide"*, Eric Tiggeler, Packt Publishing and *"Joomla! 1.5 Template Design"*, Tessa Blakeley Silver, Packt Publishing.

Installing the JomSocial component, modules, and plugins

JomSocial requires PHP5 or above for installation, therefore we need to ensure that our development server or remote server supports PHP 5 or above. You can purchase and download your professional copy of JomSocial 1.8.x from the JomSocial website (http://www.jomsocial.com/buy-now.html) or you can try it free for 30 days. Although the component is commercial, most of the add-ons have a GPL license.

The professional copy of JomSocial comprises a component, 13 modules, and 23 plugins. Some of the modules and plugins are available on the JomSocial website (http://www.jomsocial.com). Click on **Download** | **Addons** to obtain access.

JomSocial modules

The modules enable us to display features at various template positions, just like any other Joomla! module.

A brief description is as follows:

- mod_videocomments: Displays video comments.
- mod_activegroups: Displays the active groups (a great way to advertise groups).
- mod_activitystream: Displays activity stream.
- mod_datingsearch: This is designed to permit people searches for dating sites. It can also be activated for users to search for other users on the social networks.
- mod_ hellome: Provides a shortcut to user profiles.
- mod_jomsocialconnect: Allows users to connect to the JomSocial social network through their Facebook account.
- mod_latestdiscussion: Displays discussions on the site.
- mod_latestgroupwalls: Displays wall postings.
- mod_latestmembers: Displays latest members.
- mod_onlineusers: Displays users who are logged in.
- mod_photocomments: Displays comments made on pictures.
- mod_statistics: Displays user statistics (I'm not sure if we want the whole world to know that no one is visiting our site).
- mod_topmembers: This is useful if there is a lot of activity on the site and we want to showcase our busiest users.

JomSocial plugins

JomSocial plugins appear as applications in users' profiles if they are made available by the administrator. This allows users to customize their profiles and add features to them. JomSocial plugins are divided into standalone applications and integrator applications.

Standalone plugins do not need additional components to function and are part of the JomSocial system.

A detailed list of standalone plugins is as follows:

- `plg_articleactivity`: This is the activity plugin.
- `plg_authorLink`: This plugin inserts a link to the author's JomSocial profile.
- `plg_feeds`: This provides the ability to display RSS feeds in a profile.
- `plg_friendslocation`: Uses the Google Maps API to display the geographic location of friends.
- `plg_groups`: Displays groups in user profiles.
- `plg_input`: A system plugin that filters out HTML code to prevent it from being inserted into walls, discussions, and input areas. The administrator can disable this plugin if they prefer to have HTML elements.
- `plg_invite`: Allows the system to create and store invite IDs from the invitation link that is sent. The invitation ID is stored in the database after the invited person completes the registration.
- `plg_jomsocialconnect`: This plugin works with the Facebook Connect function. It is primarily used if one is having display issues in Internet Explorer 6.
- `plg_jomsocialuser`: This plugin is primarily used for administrative purposes. It removes the user from the database when the user is deleted by the administrator. It also monitors the login/logout process.
- `plg_latestphoto`: Displays users' pictures in their profiles.
- `plg_myarticles`: This displays articles authored by users in their profile.
- `plg_mycontacts`: Displays a user's contact information. If a user has other user IDs for other e-mail systems or social networks, they can use the contact application to share that information.
- `plg_mygoogleads`: Displays a user's Google ads under their profile.
- `plg_system`: Permits the performance of system-wide tasks, such as adding core applications to all profiles.
- `plg_twitter`: This displays users' tweets in their profile.
- `plg_walls`: Displays users' walls in their profile.
- `plg_wordfilter`: A system plugin to filter out inappropriate words.

Integrator applications

Integrator plugins allow other components to integrate with the social network. In this section, we will discuss one that comes with the JomSocial professional copy. `plg_fireboard` (also known as Kunena) is the integrator plugin that allows us to display forum posts in profiles, and requires use of the Kunena component.

More information about other integrator plugins can be found on the JomSocial website (`http://www.jomsocial.com/docs/`).

To install the JomSocial component, make sure that you are logged in to the Joomla administrative back-end (`http://localhost/joomla/administrator`).

For installation:

1. Click on **Extensions | Install/Uninstall**.
2. Click on **Extensions** on the top menu, and then choose **Install/Uninstall** from the drop-down menu.
3. Once the **Extensions Manager** has opened, under the **Install** option, click on **Upload Package File**, and then click on **Browse**. Locate the `com_community_pro_1.8.x.zip`, select it, and then click on **Open**.
4. Click on **Upload File & Install**.
5. If the installation is successful, we will see a screen similar to the next screenshot. Click on **Complete your installation** to finalize the installation process. Then click on **Next**, and the installer will walk us through the next steps.

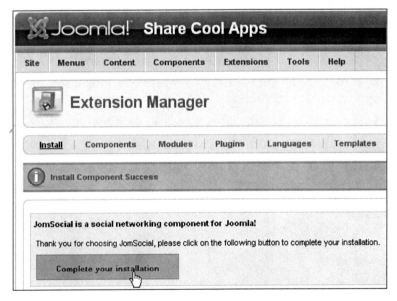

6. When the installation is complete, we will see the following screenshot:

7. Click on **Next** to view the JomSocial Component and administrative panel.

8. Congratulations, we have just installed JomSocial!

Compatible JomSocial plugins and modules are installed like any other Joomla! extension. To install the plugins and modules, follow these steps:

1. Click on **Extensions | Install/Uninstall**.

2. In the **Extensions Manager** screen, under **Upload Package File**, click on **Browse**. Locate the plugin or module that you want to install, select it, and then click on **Open**.

3. Click on **Upload File & Install**. The Joomla! administrator system will display an installation message to confirm whether the plugin or module was successfully installed or not.

4. Repeat the installation process for all required plugins and modules.

Now let us take a view of the front-end of the social networking system. JomSocial automatically creates a menu for the social network under the Joomla! main menu.

To take a peek:

1. Click on **Preview** from the administrative menu to view the front-end. If you don't have your main menu enabled, you may not see this.

2. Notice the **JomSocial** link under the main menu. Click on it to experience the first view of our network.

3. At the moment, we only have one user — the administrator. Click on the icon under **Members** to find out more about the administrator.

We have not yet added any content, so there are no activities.

The JomSocial Administrative Panel

We have successfully installed the component and previewed it from the front-end. Let's continue building our site by determining the JomSocial settings. Under configuration, we have the following features: Site, Media, Groups, Layout, Privacy, Network, Facebook, Connect, Remote Storage, and Integration. These features can be adjusted by the administrator to determine the extent of user participation and interaction.

From the administrative back-end, go to **Components | JomSocial | Configuration**, for an overview of the administrative features of the network.

Site

Following are the features of the JomSocial social networking system:

- **Reportings**: Will we encourage users to report inappropriate content to the system administrator? If yes, enter an e-mail address to which such reports should be sent.

- **Advance Search**: Will we allow guests to search our site without registering?

- **Cronjob / Scheduled Task Process**: Do we want our system to be able to send e-mails? JomSocial uses the cron job feature to send our e-mails. This is a very useful feature, and we may want to keep it activated.

- **Registrations**: Will users have to accept terms and conditions for using our site during the registration process? If yes, we need to enter terms and conditions in the edit box. Also, we need to determine whether users have to use the recaptcha function during the registration process. We will need to register for an account at http://recaptcha.net/ and enter the required codes here.

- **Frontpage**: This displays the name of our site.

- **SEO**: This allows the user to enter the preferred format for search engine optimization (SEO).

- **Social Bookmarking**: This enables or disables social bookmarking.

- **Featured Limits**: What is the maximum number of users, videos, and groups that can be featured on the site at any one time?

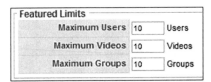

- **Messaging**: Do we want users to be able to e-mail each other? How many e-mails can they send per day?

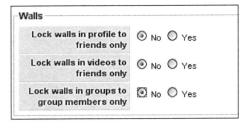

- **Walls**: What privacy settings do we want to set for users? If we select **Yes**, then only approved friends can post messages on a user's wall.

- **Time Offset (Daylight Saving Time)**: Daylight Saving Time settings are applicable to countries that usually change their time during daylight saving periods.

- **Emails**: Would we prefer the e-mails that we send out to be in HTML format or regular text format?

Media

With media comes the following features:

- **Photo Gallery**: Do we want to enable a photo gallery system? If yes, what are the settings for this feature? What will be the image dimensions, file size, and so on?

- **Videos**: Do we want to enable a video uploading system? If so, what are the settings for our uploads?

Groups

Do we want our site to have groups? **Groups** are like networks within our website, where users with similar interests can interact.

Layout

Following are the layout features:

- **Template Settings**: JomSocial comes with four templates. We will learn how to modify the templates in *Chapter 7, Customizing the JomSocial Template*.

- **Karma**: Do we want users to get points for activities on the site? This will be useful for a site that provides incentives for activities.

- **Display Settings**: How would we like our users to appear? If we have installed a specific text editor, we can also select it here as the default editor.

- **Frontpage**: How many users, videos, or groups will appear on our main networking site?

Privacy

This is used to set up default privacy settings. Users can always change their settings.

```
┌─Privacy──────────────────────────────────────────────────┐
│                                                          │
│  Default User Privacy                                    │
│                                                          │
│      Profile privacy    ⦿ Public ○ Members ○ Friends     │
│                                                          │
│      Friends privacy    ⦿ Public ○ Members ○ Friends ○ Self │
│                                                          │
│      Photos privacy     ⦿ Public ○ Members ○ Friends ○ Self │
│                                                          │
│  Default User Email & Notifications                      │
│                                                          │
│   Receive system e-mails   ○ No ⦿ Yes                    │
│                                                          │
│      Allow Applications    ○ No ⦿ Yes                    │
│                                                          │
│   Receive wall comment     ○ No ⦿ Yes                    │
│            notification                                  │
│                                                          │
└──────────────────────────────────────────────────────────┘
```

Network

Do we prefer to keep the JomSocial Company (Azrul) updated with what's happening on our site?

```
┌─JomSocial Network Configuration──────────────────────────────────────┐
│                                                                      │
│  Enable JomSocial    ⦿ No ○ Yes                                      │
│         Network                                                      │
│                                                                      │
│     Description    │App Reviews                                   │  │
│                                                                      │
│          Tags      │Find out what others are saying about cell phone apps│ │
│                                                                      │
│       Join URL     │http://localhost/joomla/index.php?option=com_community&view=register│ │
│                                                                      │
│   Update Interval  │24              │ (hours)                        │
│                                                                      │
│   Upload New Logo  │            │ [Browse...]  ☐ Replace Image       │
│                                                                      │
└──────────────────────────────────────────────────────────────────────┘
```

Facebook Connect

Do we want users to be able to log in to our social networking site with their existing Facebook accounts, and invite their friends to join our network? The site needs to be on a remote server (on the Internet) for this to work.

Facebook API Configurations		Facebook Settings	
Facebook API Key		Import facebook profile on first sign up	○ No ◉ Yes
Facebook Application Secret		Add Facebook watermarks on avatar	◉ No ○ Yes
		Automatically re-import user profile upon login	◉ No ○ Yes
		Automatically re-import user avatar upon login	◉ No ○ Yes
		Import user status from Facebook	◉ No ○ Yes

Instructions on how to set up Facebook Connect can be found in *Chapter 8, Tips and Tricks*.

Remote storage

If we decide to enable the video and photo uploads, those take up a lot of server space. We will have to determine if we prefer to store all of the materials on our hosting or on another server.

Storage Methods	
Photos	Local Server ▾
Videos	Local Server ▾

The remote server that can be used with JomSocial is Amazon S3. More about the Amazon S3 account can be found at: `http://aws.amazon.com/s3/`.

Integrations

Would we like to enable a link to MyBlog, a blogging component? We will need to install the MyBlog component (available at `http://www.azrul.com/products/my-blog.html`) before we enable this feature.

My Blog Integrations	
Enable My Blog icon in profile	◉ No ○ Yes

Click on **Save** to save our configuration settings, and then click on **Home** to return to the main JomSocial configuration page.

Users

There is one user in the community at the moment, the administrator. As an administrator, we can always come back here to view a list of users in our network.

 If you already have a Joomla!-driven website with users, the users will appear under this feature.

Custom profiles

What are our preferences in terms of the features of user profiles? Apart from registration information such as name, username, e-mail, and password, what other details will be required during registration? And what other optional features can users add?

We have four options when setting up profile features:

- **Published**: Do we want the feature published?
- **Visible**: Do we want it to be visible in their profile?
- **Required**: Is the information required for registration?
- **Registration**: Should it appear as a part of the registration process?

We can also change the order of the features.

Disabling fields that we do not want users to fill out during the registration process

Select the checkbox to enable or disable the fields. We can also click on the title to make changes to specific fields.

Num		Name	Field Code	Type	published	Visible	Required	Registration
	☐	Group: Basic Information			✓	✓	✓	✓
1	☐	Gender	FIELD_GENDER	Select	✓	⊗	✓	✓
2	☐	Birthday	FIELD_BIRTHDAY	Date	⊗	⊗	✓	✓
3	☐	About me	FIELD_ABOUTME	Textarea	✓	✓	⊗	⊗

Modifying existing groups and fields

Click on the **Group: Contact Information** title. Change the name and click on **Save** when done.

Edit Group ⊗

Create new group for your custom profiles.

Name :	Apps
published :	● Yes ○ No
Visible :	● Yes ○ No

Save   **Cancel**

Modifying field titles

To modify field titles, carry out the steps shown below:

1. Click on the field title: **Land Phone**, for example.

2. Rename the field, and make any required changes to the settings. Click on the **Save** button when you are done.

Edit Profile ⊗

Create new custom profile for your site.

Name : `Favorite apps`	published : ⦿ Yes ○ No
Type : `Textbox` ▾	Required : ○ Yes ⦿ No
Group: : `Apps` ▾	
Field Code : `FIELD_APPS`	Visible : ⦿ Yes ○ No
Registration : ○ Yes ⦿ No	
Minimum Characters : `10`	Maximum Characters : `5000`
Tooltip : `Tell us about your favorite apps`	

Save   Cancel

Creating a new group or field

Click on **New Group** or **New Field**, and then complete the requirements. When creating a new field, make sure that you assign it to a group.

Groups

Any groups that have been created can be viewed here.

Creating a new group category

What group categories will be in our network? For our site, we will create four categories, because we want groups to aggregate under four broad categories: iPhone Apps, Droid Apps, Blackberry Apps, and Other Apps.

To create a new category:

1. Click on **Group Categories** and click on **New**.
2. A form opens; enter the name and a description of the group, and then click on **Save**.

Deleting an existing group

Select the group that you want to delete, and then click on **Delete**.

Num	☐	Name	Category Description
1	☑	Automotive	Automotive groups category
2	☑	Business	Business groups category
3	☑	General	General group category.

 Use this feature with caution, especially when you have a live website with groups and users in the categories.

Editing an existing group

Click on the category that you want to edit. When the window opens, make the required changes, and then click on **Save**.

Num	☐	Name	Category Description
1	☐	iPhone apps	iPhone app groups
2	☐	Music	Music groups category

Video categories

Video categories are the types of videos that we want to have, and the categories that we want published.

Reportings

Reported activities will appear here. If we have set these up in the configuration, we will receive e-mails every time there is a report about activities on our site.

User points

Go back to the JomSocial **Home Panel** to enable Karma points. If we enabled Karma points under **Configuration | Layout**, users will get points for specific activities.

We can adjust the number of points, or enable or disable points. This can be done by identifying or creating tasks that will be awarded points. To do that:

1. Click on the user rule title **Upload Photo**.
2. Adjust the points to be awarded for this activity, and then click on **Save**.
3. Click on **Home** to return to the main JomSocial configuration page.

Upload Photo ⊗

Action String :	photo.upload
Rule Description :	Give points when registered user upload photos.
Plugin :	com_community
User Access :	Public Registered Special
published :	⦿ Yes ○ No
Points :	0

Save   Cancel

Applications

The plugins that we installed appear as applications. The applications enable users to customize and extend their profiles to include features that have been made available by the administrator. We installed 18 plugins, some of which need components to be fully functional. Some plugins also serve as bridges between other components and the social network. As we consider features for our network, we may want to keep some of them disabled until we have tested them and are ready to make them available for use.

To access applications:

1. Click on the **Applications** icon, as shown in the screenshot.

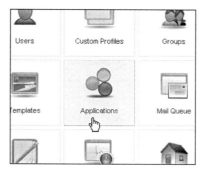

2. Click on **Click here to view the applications lists**, as shown in the screenshot.

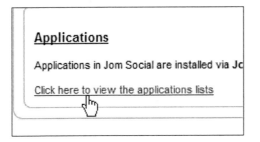

3. Notice that there are now 18 plugins. Plugins need to be enabled in order to be a part of our social network. Select the checkbox next to the currently-disabled plugins, and then click on **Enable**. We will enable five applications at this time: **Latest Photos, Feeds, Groups, Walls**, and **My twitter updates**.

#		Plugin Name	Enabled	Order ✎	Ac
1	☐	Latest Photos	✔	▼ 1	
2	☐	Feeds	✔	▲ ▼ 2	
3	☐	Groups	✔	▲ ▼ 3	
4	☐	Walls	✔	▲ ▼ 4	
5	☐	My twitter updates	✔	▲ ▼ 5	
6	☐	My Google Ads	⊗	▲ ▼ 6	

Filter: [ ] Go Reset

Modifying plugin parameters

The plugins (or applications, as they appear in user profiles) can be adjusted. We can change the names. We (the administrators) can also make applications permanent features of user profiles, or we can give users the option to enable or disable them.

For modification:

1. Click on the **Walls** plugin to edit it. Notice that it is currently enabled.

```
Details
                Name:  Walls
             Enabled:  ○ No  ◉ Yes
                Type:  community
         Plugin File:  walls                    .php
        Access Level:  Public
                       Registered
                       Special
               Order:  0 (Walls) ▼
         Description:  Walls for JomSocial © AzrulStudio 2008
```

2. Under **Parameters** (on the right-hand side), notice that we have the option to make it a core application, that is, a permanent fixture of user profiles. We want to make this a core feature.

3. Set a character limit on wall posts, and then click on **Save**.

In review, we have gained an overview of the administrative features of our social network. As an administrator, we can always return to the administrative panel to make adjustments as needed.

Linking to the social network

Earlier in the chapter, we saw that JomSocial automatically creates a link to the social network. In this section, we will demonstrate how to unpublish the link (if you are not yet ready to publish your network), modify the name of the existing link, or create a new link (if you want to have the link on a different menu).

Modifying an existing menu

Let's rename the JomSocial link and call it **Sign Up--Become a Reviewer**.

1. From the administrative back-end of Joomla, click on **Menus | Main Menu**.

2. Click on **JomSocial**.

3. Change the **Title** and **Alias**, and then click on **Save** when done. The Alias has to be lowercase with no space in between. Use a "dash" or "underscore" to create space. This is essential for SEO (Search Engine Optimization).

```
┌─Menu Item Details ──────────────────────────────────┐
│                                                       │
│              ID:  2                                   │
│                                                       │
│           Title:  Sign Up - - Become a Reviewer       │
│                                                       │
│           Alias:  sign-up                             │
│                                                       │
│            Link:  index.php?option=com_community      │
│                                                       │
│      Display in:  Main Menu  ▼                        │
└───────────────────────────────────────────────────────┘
```

4. Click on **Preview** again, and notice that the JomSocial link has now changed to **Sign Up--Become a Reviewer**.

5. While we are here, we want to change the name of the **Home** menu to **Howdy!**.

6. Save your changes, refresh the site, and view the page from the front-end.

 The location of our menu may depend on our adopted template or theme, and where we want to put it.

The social network

We have installed the social network, added plugins for content integration, and changed the menu name. Let's go to our main page (http://localhost/joomla/) and click on the **Sign Up--Become a Reviewer** link, as follows.

Congratulations! We have just set up our first social network.

Summary

In this chapter, we learned how to install and configure the JomSocial component for social networking. We then installed the plugins and modules that came with our professional JomSocial package. These plugins will be used to extend and enhance the social networking experience on our site. However, in order to realize the full potential of our social network, we need to migrate our site to a remote server for a live and real-time experience.

Our next chapter will begin with the migration of our site from the localhost to a remote server. We will then begin the process of making our site interactive, by creating and managing a user profile.

3
Remote Installation and Managing User Profiles

In the earlier chapters, we set up our social networking site locally. We also gained some insightful knowledge about the configuration of JomSocial as a Joomla! add-on. We now need to migrate our site to a remote server, in order to make our site live for further development. This is absolutely important because we intend to integrate our site with existing social networking sites such as Facebook and Twitter, and this cannot be done in a local environment. Those of us wanting to continue development locally can continue to do so, especially if we do not have a registered domain name and hosting account. We can use the backup process in this chapter to migrate our site when we are ready to go live.

In this chapter, we will learn how to:

- Migrate the site from a local machine to a remote server by:
    - Backing up the local site using a Joomla! backup system called Akeeba Backup (formerly known as JoomlaPack)
    - Creating a live website from the backup

- Sign up for an account
- Manage user profiles by:
    - Editing user profiles
    - Changing profile pictures
    - Setting profile privacy
    - Adding applications and privacy settings for applications

- Delete a profile

Migrating the site from a local to remote server

We have reached the stage in the development of our social network where we will migrate our site to a remote host. The migration process involves backing up our entire site, downloading the backup files, and then using them to restore our site in a different hosting environment. This same backup process can be used for routine backups of a Joomla! site as a security measure. It can also be used for the restoration of a site or for switching a site from an old to a new hosting account. These processes are invaluable to a Joomla! website developer.

Backing up the local site using Akeeba Backup

Following are the steps necessary to create an Akeeba Backup:

1. Download Akeebabackup and the `kickstart.php` script from the AkeebaBackup website: `http://www.akeebabackup.com/download.html`.

    The Kickstart download is a `.zip` package. We will have to extract the files to access the `kickstart.php` file.

2. Install the Akeebabackup component through the regular Joomla! extension installation process. Akeebabackup is designed to back up the entire website, including database data and website configuration.

3. Configure the Akeebabackup component by going to **Components | Akeebabackup | Configuration**.

Basic Configuration	
Output Directory	C:\xampp\htdocs\joomla\adm Browse...
Temporary Directory	C:\xampp\htdocs\joomla\tmp Browse...
Log Level	All Information and Debug
Backup archive name	site-[HOST]-[DATE]-[TIME]
Backup Type	Full site backup

Advanced configuration	
Database backup engine	Native MySQL backup engine Configure...
Filesystem scanner engine	Smart scanner Configure...
Archiver engine	ZIP format Configure...
Data processing engine	No post-processing Configure...
File writing engine	
Embedded restoration script	Akeeba Backup Installer
Virtual directory for off-site files	external_files

Quota management		
Enable size quota		
Size quota		15.00 Mb
Enable count quota		
Count quota		3.00

Fine tuning		
Minimum execution time		2.00 s
Maximum execution time		14.00 s
Execution time bias		75.00 %

As shown in the previous screenshot, most of the default settings work well. We should pay attention to the **Output Directory** and the **Archiver engine**. The **Output Directory** is the folder where the backup will be saved; this can be changed if necessary. Take note of this directory, as we will download the archived file after backing up the site. The **Archiver engine** determines the backup format. The JPA format is recommended for backing up from a Linux environment and restoring it also in a Linux environment.

We used **ZIP format** for our backup. Akeeba comes with detailed instructions that can be found in the documentation files. More information can be found on the Akeeba Backup website: `http://www.akeebabackup.com/documentation/index.html`.

4. Click on **Backup Now** to prepare for the backup. This step allows us to name the backup and provide a description of it. We will keep the defaults here. Click on the **Backup Now** button (on the right) to initiate the backup process. The duration of the backup depends on the size of the website.

Akeeba Backup:: Backup Now

⁝ Please do not browse to another page unless you see a completion or error message.

Backup Progress

✔ Initializing backup process
✔ Embedding the installer in the archive
✔ Backing up databases
➡ Backing up files
   Finalizing the backup process

C:/xampp/htdocs/joomla/templates/ja_purity/css

Last server response 7s ago

5. We will see the following message if the backup process is successful. Click on **Administer Backup Files** to download the ZIP file.

Akeeba Backup:: Backup Now

Backup Completed Successfully

✔ Congratulations! The backup process has completed successfully. You can now navigate to another page.

Administer Backup Files

View Log

Creating a live website from the backup

Akeeba Backup provides us with a seamless process for restoring websites from backups. The restoration process requires the backup file and a hosting environment, that meets the Joomla! installation requirements. But before we restore our site, we need to log in to our remote server and create a database. To run the restoration, we will need the database name, server information (this could be localhost or a unique hostname), and a database username and password. Make sure that the database user has been assigned all privileges on the database.

We have purchased a hosting account from `http://www.hostmonster.com` and, as we can see from the following screenshot, the domain is parked. **Hostmonster** has a good array of open source and proprietary software. One of our favorite **Hostmonster** services is **Simplescript**, which is accessible through the **Hostmonster Cpanel**. This service simplifies the installation and upgrade processes of a select number of open source software applications.

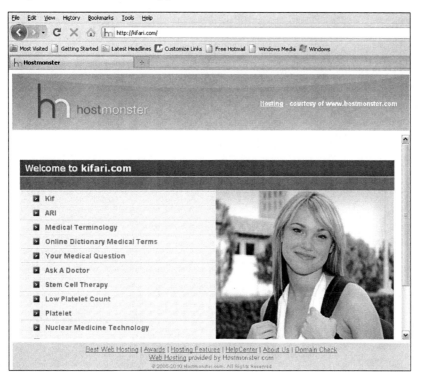

Let's create a live site from the local backup:

1. Upload the `Akeebabackup.zip` file (site backup file) and the `kickstart.php` file into the root folder of our hosting account. The remote root folder could be `public_html`, `www`, `htdocs`, or a sub-folder, depending on the hosting setup. The upload of the `Akeebabackup.zip` (site backup file) and the `kickstart.php` files can be done by using the **Control Panel** of the hosting account, or through an **FTP (File Transfer Protocol)** client such as FileZilla. FileZilla is an open source FTP client that can be downloaded from the official website: `http://filezilla-project.org/`.

Filename /	Filesize	Filetype	Last modified	Permissions	Owner/Group
..					
kickstart.php	107,564	PHP Script	3/14/2010 6:38...	0644	953 954
site-localhost-2010...	11,514,849	Compresse...	3/14/2010 6:40...	0644	953 954

2. Run the `kickstart.php` script by browsing to the site address, for instance, `http://www.yourwebsite.com/kickstart.php`—in our case, this is `http://www.kifari.com/kickstart.php`. This will activate the website's restoration wizard online. Keep the default settings and click on **Start**, as illustrated in the following screenshot. The wizard will walk us through the extraction of the backup files, and complete the migration process. We are not using **FTP Options**, so we will not put any information in here. Click on **Start**, and let the wizard do its thing.

JoomlaPack Kickstart 2.4.1

Backup Archive

Please select a ZIP/JPA file below and press the "Start" button.
/site-localhost-20100314-221227.zip ▼

    Start

Operation Method

⦿ AJAX (refreshless) ○ JavaScript Redirects

Extraction Method

⦿ Write directly to files ○ Use FTP
☐ Restore file/directory permissions (JPA archives only)

FTP Options

Host	localhost
Port	21
Username	
Password	
Initial Directory	/

Stealth Mode

Stealth mode (restrict access only to your IP while restoring)   ☐
Stealth Mode redirection URL
(or leave blank to display a 403 Forbidden message to non authorized users)

Fine Tuning

Maximum archive chunk to process per step (Bytes)   1048756

3. The wizard will prompt us to enter the correct details as needed. We will be required to enter the database name, hostname, database username, and password. If the installation is successful, we will be prompted to remove the installation directory.

 Although the system provides a link to remove the installation directory, we need to check the root folder to make sure that the installation folder has been deleted. We may need to manually remove the folder.

4. Our website address is `http://www.kifari.com`; browse to this address.

![App Reviews - Mozilla Firefox browser window showing the Kifari App Reviews website with navigation links Howdy!, Sign Up, Become a Reviewer, and Scroll To Top]

5. Congratulations! We have migrated our site from the local server to a remote server. Note that our site is restored with its configuration, and administrator username and password intact.

 We do not have to install Joomla! for the migration process. The backup file contains all of the necessary files for the complete migration of the website from the local server to the remote server. Once the backup has been installed, we will have the same Joomla! version as we did when the backup was created.

In review, we have restored our development website on a remote server by using the Joomla! backup and restoration component Akeebabackup.

Signing up for an account

It is important to understand the user profile settings as a way of determining what tools are available to users to facilitate their interaction with others in the network. It is also important to know how the features that we enabled in the previous chapter will affect our users. Also, as an administrator we have to understand that interaction among site users depends on how we configure the site, especially in terms of the default user profile settings and the applications that we make available to the users.

Let's create a new profile, by signing up for an account:

1. Click on **Sign Up--Become a Reviewer**.
2. Sign up for an account by clicking on **JOIN US NOW, IT'S FREE**.

3. Enter the required registration information, and then click on **Next**. Notice that some of the information is marked with an asterix (*) alongside it. This means that those fields are required. Complete the requirements as set by the administrator.

The registration process also encourages us to upload our image or avatar. We can skip this process and change our image later. We may want to pay attention to the maximum file size and width of the image that we can upload. The maximum file size for uploads that shows here is the maximum size defined in the `php.ini` file. Do you recall that in the previous chapter, we set the maximum image upload size to 8 MB? This means that users cannot upload images larger than 8 MB.

4. After we click on **Skip**, we will get a message stating that an activation link has been sent to our e-mail account. This serves as a verification of the account and an anti-spam mechanism. If we want users to start working on their profile without activating their account, the settings can be changed from the administrative back-end by going to **Site | Global Configurations | System | User settings**.

User Registered.

Your account has been created and an activation link has been sent to the e-mail address you entered. You must activate the account by clicking on the activation link in the email sent before you can login.

5. Click on the **Sign Up--Become a Reviewer** link. Notice that there are now two users in the system.

Managing an account

In this section, we are going to manage a user profile by editing the profile, changing profile pictures and profile privacy settings, and adding applications and privacy settings for those applications.

Editing the user profile

We have to log in and view the new user's profile, Jackie Newperson's profile. In our case, it is the account we created:

1. Enter your login information.

There are some links below the **Login** button, in case we (users) forget our username or password or would like the activation code to be resent to our e-mail. We can use these links to make a request, and the system will send us the information. This applies only to a remote and not a locally hosted installation.

2. After logging in, the **Profile** menu is the first one we'll see.

The Profile menu is divided into four sections, as follows:

- **Section 1**: This is a brief section that shows our image or avatar, and shows when we became a member, when we were last online, and how many people have viewed the profile.

- **Section 2**: This section shows the information that we specified during the registration process. Click on the pen icon to edit this information.

- **Section 3**: This section contains an image of the "typical" menu items that may be frequently used by users. This is a quick access panel to key menu items that are also available under the menu items—**Home, Profile, Friends, Applications**, and **Inbox**. Under **My Status** you can share your regular thoughts about how you feel, or your status updates. Once you start typing in there, the box becomes editable; click on **Save** when you are done.

- **Section 4**: User activities and plugins (or applications) appear here.

In review, we have just logged in and viewed the first interface of our profile. Let the fun begin! In the following steps, we are going to manage our profile by changing the picture, and editing our profile, our details, and our profile privacy settings. We will also learn how to delete our profiles if we are no longer interested in being a part of this network.

Changing the profile picture

Follow these steps to change our profile picture:

1. Click on **Change profile picture**.

2. Users can always change their profile image. Click on **Browse** to locate the image that you want to use, and then click on **Upload**, to upload it to your profile. Notice the image size limit of the following images. The size limit can be changed by the administrator under the configuration section of our social network.

3. Congratulations, we have just uploaded a new profile image. We look great!

4. Click on the **Profile** link and notice that we have a new image. The system resizes your image to meet configuration settings and requirements, and creates a thumbnail.

We can edit some of the details entered during the registration process such as our name and password. To edit our details:

1. Click on **Profile | Edit details**.

2. Click on **Save** when done. We cannot change our username, as shown in the following screenshot.

Setting profile privacy settings

The default privacy settings are set to public. The administrator sets the default settings; however, users can opt to keep or change these default privacy settings.

We also have the option to determine the types of e-mails that we receive. We can choose to receive or not receive administrator e-mails that concern network members, notification changes to applications, and wall comments when users comment on our walls.

The **Preferences** section allows us to choose the number of activities that should appear on our profile at any given time. If it's more than the specified number, only the latest activities will appear.

Customizing our activities with applications

We have configured our profile. Let's customize it by adding applications to it. Without applications, visitors to the network or our friends cannot see what we do or what our interests are.

- Click on **Applications**. There are two groups of applications: **Core Applications** and **Your Installed Applications**.

- The **Core Applications** are applications that have been installed by the administrator and are a part of the network. Users do not have the option to remove core applications.

- **Your Installed Applications** are those applications that users can install themselves, based on what has been made available by the administrator. In the previous chapter, we installed some plugins. These plugins become the applications that users can add to their profile.

To add some applications to our profile:

1. Click on **Browse**.
2. Identify your preferred applications and add them. After adding an application, the system will notify us that an application has been added. Some applications may have settings to configure. It is always important to click on **Settings** to see whether additional configuration is needed.

3. Click on **My Applications** to view all of the applications that we have installed.
4. We can click on **Remove** to remove applications that we have added, but we cannot disable core applications.
5. Each application has privacy settings. Click on **Privacy** to view the privacy options for an application.

We have managed our profile by uploading a new image, changing the settings, and adding applications in order to personalize our profile. It is essential to note that our activites are logged under our profile and on the main page of the network. This provides visitors to our site with updates of reviews and user activites, and encourages non-members to join the site.

Deleting a profile

The **Profile** menu also gives us the option to delete our profile. If we do not like our profile and would like to either create a new one or just get out of the network, this gives us the opportunity to do that. Profile deletions cannot be reversed. The **Delete Profile** link can be found under any of the sub-menus under the profile.

Change profile picture	Edit profile	Edit details	Privacy	Preferences		Delete Profile

Summary

In this chapter, we learned how to migrate our site from a local machine to a remote host. We created a profile, configured its settings, uploaded new avatars, and added applications. We now have a good insight into the details of a user account. This should help us as administrators to develop this network to meet the needs of the network's users. We are now ready to interact with others.

4
Making Connections with Users and Friends

In *Chapter 1*, *Not Another Social Networking Site*, we shared an example of how connections enabled the MIT team to win the DARPA challenge. The team, through their online network, received reports on balloon sightings. The team positioned itself to be able to connect to others, and benefited from the networks of those connected to them.

Social networks are changing the way information is disseminated. They are helping individuals to customize information for their personal use. Through social networks, personalized content can easily be accessed by others, or by a group of friends, on a social networking site. As the interaction and exchanges on social networks become more intense, more social networking sites have emerged all over the world.

Social networks are diverse, but they all focus on facilitating communication among users who freely share information and resources. This information ranges from personal user information, news, products and services, and in some cases, the rating of goods and services, and the offering of donations.

A social network has to be user-centered, and needs to facilitate the generation of personalized information about oneself or other issues, or products or services that are of interest to users. In setting up our social networking site, we have to identify the kind of unique information sharing system that will enable our users to generate their own content, and be able to disseminate their information with a degree of control over how the information is shared, and who gets to see or use the information that our users post.

In our quest to build a site that facilitates some form of information sharing on cell phone applications, the key questions are:

- What will make our service attractive to users?
- How can we distinguish our social networking environment and activities from other Social Network Services (SNSes)?

These are issues that we need to consider, and address in the form of a detailed plan, before we embark on a social networking project.

It is important not to lose sight of the reality that social networks are a trend in the communication industry that point to the evolving nature of human communication. Human communication is, and continues to be, a complex and multidimensional flow and exchange of information. Social networks are a manifestation of this complex and multidimensional phenomena. Social networking is primarily about establishing relationships and the sharing of information among individuals with similar interests. Also, it has evolved to facilitate the sharing of information or interaction between institutions and people of interest.

In the previous chapter, we learned how to create a profile. In this chapter, we will start making connections with people by doing the following:

- Creating test users
- Making connections with other users within the network
- Writing and checking our e-mails
- Inviting other people to the network

Creating test users

We currently have only two users in our network. We need more members to be able to make connections. One way to create more users is to repeat the steps laid out in *Chapter 3, Remote Installation and Managing User Profiles*. However, as web developers, we have other options to generate users for testing purposes.

After migrating our site to a remote host, we need to know how our users will interact with each other. The foobla Users Generator (or JLord Users Generator) is a Joomla! component that provides us with the ability to generate users for testing purposes. The component can be found under the Joomla! extensions on the Joomla! website: `http://extensions.joomla.org`. Click on **Communities & Groupware | User Management | Users Generator** to access the component. You can visit the official foobla website to download the component at `http://foobla.com/products/free-joomla-extensions/foobla-users-generator-for-joomla.html`.

We will create test users through the following steps:

1. Download the JLord Users Generator component.
2. Install the component through the Joomla! extension installer on the administrative back-end.
3. Go to **Components | JLord Generator** to generate users. The interface is intuitive, and the default settings work well.

The **Manual** option provides administrators with the option to set a specific naming sequence for usernames, passwords, and e-mails. The **Manual** option also provides administrators with the opportunity to decide which users should be activated, and the group to which they belong (if we have set up groups).

4. After we receive the message that the process is complete, click on **User Manager** to see generated users.

Processing finished!

Total : 50

SUCCESSFUL : 50

Fail : 0

| User Manager | Come back and Get more fun! |

JLord Generator 1.5.0.2 (You are using latest version!).

There are now 50 users with unique IDs and unique (non-existent) e-mails on our website. If we keep the defaults, we may not know what the passwords are. For testing purposes, we will create a few new passwords to match the usernames.

User Details

Name	jlord_test_user103
Username	jlord_test_user103
E-mail	jlord_test_user103@yahoo.com
New Password	••••••••••••••••••
Verify Password	••••••••••••••••••

Group	Public Front-end
	  - Registered
	    - Author
	     - Editor
	      - Publisher
	- Public Back-end
	  - Manager
	    - Administrator
	     - Super Administrator

Block User	⦿ No ○ Yes
Receive System E-mails	⦿ No ○ Yes
Register Date	2008-12-26 20:17:04
Last Visit Date	2008-12-30 04:41:36

Let's view our website to see how many users appear on our network:

1. Click on **Sign up--Become a reviewer** from the front-end.

> Notice that we now have 23 active members on our site. Although we had created 50 members, only 23 were activated. This is designed to mimic how users will behave on a site. Many will create accounts but few will become active.

2. Click on **View all members** to view the members.

3. If user profiles are public, visitors to the site can browse profiles to see users' interests and activities. Testing how connections will occur is always important before opening the site to others.

Making connections

We logged in as some of the users and used the process laid out in the previous chapter to upload some profile images. Let's click on **View all members** again. It looks like there are some appheads (active registered member of the site) in there, and they have snail avatars. Click on a username (for example, **jlord_test_user103**).

Jackie Newperson
Oh, what a beautiful morning
0 friends   Write Message   Add as friend

Administrator
0 friends   Write Message   Add as friend

jlord_test_user103
0 friends   Write Message   Add as friend

jlord_test_user74
0 friends   Write Message   Add as friend

jlord_test_user105
0 friends   Write Message   Add as friend

Let's make some connections by logging in as one of the test users:

1. Find a user that we want to connect to. If their profile is public, we can browse to see what they have been up to, and if we are interested in establishing a connection, we should click on **Add as friend**.

2. As we are already logged in, a message box will appear and we can type in our introductory message, and then click on **Add Friend**.

If a user is not logged in but wants to make friends, they will be required to create an account and log in before they can make any connections. Only active registered members can make connections.

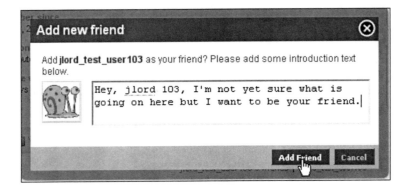

3. Log out and log in as a different user (such as Test User 103) to determine if we have received any notifications.

4. After we log in, notice the bell on our Inbox tab on the menu—click on it.

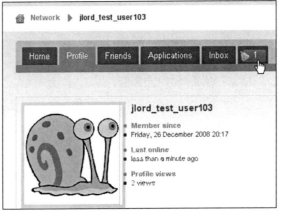

5. We can find out who this person is and then approve their request. After approving the request and refreshing the page, notice that **jlord_test_user68** and **jlord_test_user103** are now friends; they appear under each other's profile.

Making or rejecting friend requests is straightforward, and users on our site can figure this out. As administrators, we now know that the tool for making and rejecting friends on our network works. Although we do not have any content at this time, we do know that people can connect, and that our website has the potential to facilitate user registration and allow users to interact with each other.

Messaging—writing and checking mails

Making connections and becoming friends with users in the network requires sending a message to a potential friend who is a user on the social networking site. The message received by the potential friend gives the user the option to accept or reject the invitation. We do not have the option to send a message back and communicate with the originator of the friend request before accepting or rejecting the invitation to be friends. It is essential to note that, like most social networking systems, communication among users on our site can only occur among users who choose to connect or become friends. This is a safety measure that helps us prevent unwanted messages.

Users can send private messages to each other within the system. Our system is designed to permit messaging only between friends.

To send a message:

1. Click on the friend to whom you want to send a message. (You must be logged in to send messages.)
2. Click on **Write Message**, as shown in the following screenshot.

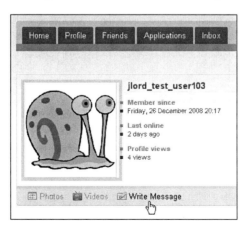

3. Type a message, and then click on the **Submit** button to send your message.

4. When the friend receives the message, they will see the notification bell (similar to the one that we saw when we sent a friend request).

5. After we click on the notification bell, we will see our message. Read the message and respond to it (if required). The messaging system can also be accessed through the **Inbox** on the **Profile** menu.

6. The messaging has begun!

Inviting others to join the network

So far, we have made connections with people who are members of the site. We assumed that everyone knows about the site and wants to make connections with people within the site. What about our friends in our e-mail address book, or our friends on other networks? They know us but do not know that we have created this new website, which is soon to be a household name!

JomSocial enables us to invite other people to our network by sending them an e-mail through the JomSocial mailing system. This process is two-fold. The administrator has to enable the function and make sure that it works, and then users can invite other people to their network.

Administrator settings

JomSocial uses an inbuilt cron job feature to send our e-mails, convert videos into .swf formats, and generally optimize the site's performance. This cron job feature has to be enabled in order to allow users to invite others outside our network by using their e-mail addresses.

To enable the cron job, carry out the steps below:

1. Log in to the back-end.
2. Click on **Components | JomSocial | Configuration**.
3. Enable the **Cronjob / Scheduled Task Process**.

Advance Search	
Allow guests to perform advance search	⦿ No ○ Yes

Cronjob / Scheduled Task Process	
Send email on page load	○ No ⦿ Yes

Registrations

4. Click on **Save**.

Enabling the cron jobs will allow users to invite others to our network. Let's see how this works.

 Some hosting services (for example, those using cPanel) may also have cron job features, which could help improve the site's performance. Check with your hosting service.

Inviting others to our network

Once the cron jobs are set up, registered users on our site can invite non-member friends to check out this new site.

Let's log in from the front-end and go through the process:

1. Log in as one of the users (Jackie Newperson).

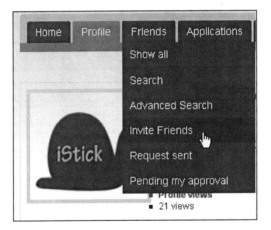

2. After logging in, go to **Friends | Invite Friends**.

3. Complete the form. We can enter as many e-mail addresses as we like, and a brief, optional message.

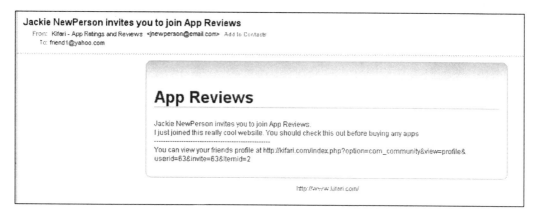

4. When we click on **Send Invite**, the system will send e-mails to the listed e-mail addresses. The recipients can then click on the link to visit our site. Below is a copy of the e-mail received by our friends.

The ability to inform others about our site and invite them to join it is a great way to connect with our friends and acquaintances in other online realms.

Summary

Making connections with friends, and communicating with other users, is the core of any online social networking community. The intuitive interface of our system makes it easy for users to know where and how to access the features of our network. Making connections is the first step in building a network.

In this chapter, we explored some of the basic interaction that occurs between users on a social networking site. In our next chapter, we will continue with this exciting experience by adding content and encouraging others to comment on our content.

5
Creating Content and Sharing Activities

A website (social network) is only as good as its content. You can have the flashiest, most gimmick-filled website, but if it does not have content, is not user friendly, and does not attract users to come back to it, then it will become another nine-day wonder and no one will remember it.

Let's take a look at some of the existing social networks and what makes people come back over and over and over again. Yelp (`http://www.yelp.com/`) is a social networking site that includes reviews of local businesses and attractions. Users can post reviews of businesses, and through a reputation system, the website ensures that only honest feedback is provided. Users to the site can also view reviews to help them decide how to approach an attraction or business. This is a great tool for planning a vacation or even for searching for good deals on goods and services within our community.

`Pleaserobme.com` is another controversial social networking site that harnesses and consolidates tweets on the site, in order to broadcast a person's absence from their abode. Like `foursquare.com`, it is designed for users to use their tweets to check in with their followers to let them know where they are. Examples of some of the tweets found on the website are: "We don't know about you, but we like to travel incognito" and "We wouldn't want the world to know where we are and what we are doing."

`Pleaserobme.com` has received so much media and blogging publicity as people criticize the fact that it may encourage burglars to rob users. Well, anyone that uses the site probably knows what the potential consequences are. The publicity, however, has been great for the developers of the site. The site has good traffic and a steady stream of site visitors. They are currently searching for venture capitalists to help them take the website to the next level.

We want our website (http://www.kifari.com) to be the next most discussed thing in the blogosphere. We stated in *Chapter 1, Not Another Social Networking Site* that our website is a social networking site that lists and reviews cell phone applications. Cell phone applications are currently grouped into Apple and Droid apps, and one needs to visit a specific brand or cell phone company site to find out more about these applications. The Apple store provides product overviews of their apps and identifies staff picks and the pick of the week. There are also some customer reviews. A rating system for Droid apps with any of the mobile phone companies is yet to be set up by any of the cell phone companies.

The idea here is to set up a social networking system that will offer a system for rating iPhone and Droid apps that is independent of the companies that sell or manufacture these products. The site is aimed at providing an open and transparent social networking environment for the exchange of listings and reviews. This information sharing and rating system will provide users with a platform on which to showcase what they have done or can do with the specific apps they have on their phones.

The information from this network could provide app developers with insightful information about specific apps. And it could help provide users and potential buyers with valuable information regarding product capabilities and limitations. Such a service has the potential to provide users with information and thereby offer potential users of specific apps the opportunity to make informed purchases. It may also provide developers with insight to product capabilities and limitations, which could be used to improve existing products or facilitate the creation of new apps.

In this chapter, we are going to create content for our site in order to attract more appheads (the name for users of our site) by:

- Extending our social network to include a ratings system by using SOBI, a Joomla! directory extension
- Listing apps
- Reviewing apps
- Displaying listings in profiles
- Sharing multimedia content such as videos and pictures

Installing SOBI2

SOBI is a free GPL Joomla! component that allows for the creation of professional directory and review systems for Joomla!-driven sites. And it integrates seamlessly with JomSocial through the requisite plugins. SOBI can be downloaded from the official website, at `http://www.sigsiu.net`. To perform this installation and integration, we will need the following:

- **SOBI2** for Joomla! 1.5 (`com_sobi2-RC2.9.2.4.j15`).

- The **Latest Reviews Module** (`SOBI2_LatestReviewed_Module`). We may need to unzip this file and upload the one for Joomla! 1.5.

- The **Latest Entries Module** (`SOBI2_Latest_Module`). We may also need to unzip this file and upload the one for Joomla! 1.5.

- The SOBI2 **Reviews & Ratings Plugin** (`reviews_plugin`), this should be the one compatible with SOBI2 (2.9.x). This plugin should be installed through the SOBI2 plugin system, and not through the regular Joomla! extension installation system.

- A plugin to integrate SOBI2 with JomSocial, which can be found on the JomSocial website (under **Addons**). The **My SOBI2 Entries** plugin will enable users to display their listings under their profile (`plg_sobiposts-0.2.zip`).

The SOBI2 component, modules, and plugins are installed just like any other Joomla! extension. As with similar Joomla! components, it is always good to configure the extension before using it. To configure SOBI, we need to do the following:

1. Go to the administrative back-end, and then click on **Components | SOBI2 | General Configuration**. Most of the default configuration settings work well.

2. The SOBI2 Configuration has various options, namely:

    - **Custom Fields Manager**: This allows us to edit, add, or remove information fields that we want users to include in their entries.

    - **General Configuration**: Some of the notable features that we may want to change under **General Configuration** include the **Component Name**, which will be the name of our directory. We will name ours "Rate, Share and Review Apps". The other thing would be **how many entries per line**; the default is 1; this can always be changed depending on the intended final look.

    - **Entry Configuration**: These settings define how we want entries to be categorized. This also includes an option to charge a fee for entries. All our entries are free.

- **View Configuration**: This includes how we want entries to appear.
- **Payment Options**: If users are charged, this provides options for payment.
- **Language Manager**: This comprises of the languages that we want to use on the site.
- **Registry Editor**: Leave it as it is.
- **Recount Categories**: To re-count how many categories are available.
- **Uninstall SOBI2**: To uninstall SOBI2.

3.   We also want to categorize apps by phone type, such as Droid, Apple, Blackberry, or Others, with other broad categories such as games, business, books, music, shopping, fitness, and so forth.

4.   Click on **Entries & Categories | Add Category**. We can also add brief descriptions of each category. Here are the categories that we have created.

5. Click on **Configuration | Custom Fields Manager**. This allows us to customize the types of reviews and items that we want users to write about on our site. Our listings will include:

   - Name of the app
   - Cost
   - Brief description of what it does

6. In the end, users will have the ability to select the categories that the app belongs to. We can specify that users can put in apps up to five categories, or whatever the settings may determine.

7. Now, let's install the SOBI2 ratings and review system. This is done through the **SOBI Configuration | Plugins | Plugin Manager**. Install the reviews plugin.

8. Click on the plugin to configure it. Towards the end of the configuration settings, there are additional things that need to be done to the code. This shows us different files where we need to insert specific codes.

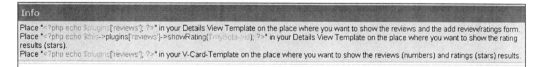

9. Let's take the first line, and break it down:

   Place "<?php echo $plugins['reviews']; ?>" in your Details View Template on the place where you want to show the reviews and the add review/ ratings form.

This is telling us to place the part in quotes **<?php echo $plugins['reviews'];
?>"** in a specific template called **Details View Template**. To do that:

- ° First, save this configuration.
- ° Go to **Templates & CSS**, and then click on the **Details View
  Template**, as illustrated in the following screenshot.

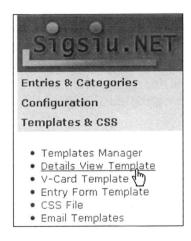

10. This will open the editable code of the **Details View Template**. (Note that the
    Details View Template is what appears after users complete the forms list
    apps). This will make a review link appear on each entry. We want the form
    to appear at the end of the description.

```php
<?php
/**
* @version $Id: sobi2.details.tmpl.php 5379 2010-02-26 17:30:01Z
Sigrid Suski $
* @package: Sigsiu Online Business Index 2
* ========================================================
* @author
* Name: Sigrid & Radek Suski, Sigsiu.NET GmbH
* Email: sobi[at]sigsiu.net
* Url: http://www.sigsiu.net
* ========================================================
* @copyright Copyright (C) 2006 - 2010 Sigsiu.NET GmbH (http://
www.sigsiu.net). All rights reserved.
* @license see http://www.gnu.org/licenses/old-licenses/gpl-
2.0.html GNU/GPL.
* You can use, redistribute this file and/or modify
* it under the terms of the GNU General Public License as
```

```
published by
* the Free Software Foundation.
*/

/*please do not remove this line */
defined( '_SOBI2_' ) || ( trigger_error("Restricted access", E_
USER_ERROR) && exit() );

/* ------------------------------------------------------------
 * This is the template for the Details View
 * ------------------------------------------------------------
 */
?>
<?php HTML_SOBI::renewal( $config,$mySobi ); ?>
<table class="sobi2Details" <?php echo $style; ?> >
  <tr>
    <td><?php echo $ico; ?><h1><?php echo $mySobi->title; ?></
h1></td>
  </tr>
  <tr>
    <td><?php echo $img; ?></td>
  </tr>
  <tr>
    <td><?php HTML_SOBI::showGoogleMaps($mySobi, $config); ?></td>
  </tr>
  <tr>
    <td>
      <div id="sobi2outer">
        <?php HTML_SOBI::waySearchUrl( $waySearchLink,$config );
?>
        <?php echo HTML_SOBI::customFieldsData( $fieldsFormatted
);?>
       <br />
      </div>
    </td>
  </tr>
</table>
<table class="sobi2DetailsFooter" width="100%">
  <tr>
    <td>
    <?php HTML_SOBI::addedDate($config,$mySobi); ?>
        
    <?php HTML_SOBI::showHits($config,$mySobi);?>
    </td>
    <td><?php HTML_SOBI::editButtons($config,$mySobi); ?></td>
  </tr>
</table>
<?php echo $plugins['reviews']; ?>
```

11. Place **"<?php echo $this->plugins['reviews']->showRating($mySobi->id); ?>"** in your **Details View Template** on the place where you want to show the rating results (stars).

12. We want this to appear alongside the title:

```
?>
<?php HTML_SOBI::renewal( $config,$mySobi ); ?>

<table class="sobi2Details" <?php echo $style; ?> >
  <tr>
    <td><?php echo $ico; ?><h1><?php echo $mySobi->title; ?></h1> <?php echo
$this->plugins['reviews']->showRating($mySobi->id); ?></td>
  </tr>
```

13. Save and go to the **V-Card Template**.

14. Place **"<?php echo $plugins['reviews']; ?>"** in your **V-Card-Template** on the place where you want to show the reviews (numbers) and ratings (stars) results.

```
<td <?php echo $style; ?>>

  <?php echo $editButton; ?>
  <?php echo $deleteButton; ?>
  <?php echo $ico; ?>
  <?php echo $img; ?>

  <?php echo $title; ?>
  <?php echo $plugins['reviews']; ?>
  <?php echo HTML_SOBI::customFieldsData($fieldsFormatted); ?>
```

15. We placed the code below the title.

16. We saved any changes that we made.

Comprehensive documentation is available on the SOBI2 website (http://www.sigsiu.net/).

After setting up SOBI2, we need to activate the SOBI2's JomSocial plugins, similar to activating any plugin. This can be done by clicking on **Components | JomSocial | Applications**.

#		Plugin Name	Enabled	Order	Access Level	Type
1	☐	Walls	✓	▼ 0	Public	community
2	☐	My SOBI Entries	✓	▲ ▼ 0	Public	community
3	☐	Latest Photos	✓	▲ ▼ 1	Public	community

We will rename **My SOBI Entries** to **My Listings**.

Because the main goal of this site is for users to provide app reviews, we will make **My Listings** part of the core profile applications (that is, all users will have this as part of their core profile, and cannot remove it).

A Joomla! component cannot be used without a link to it. So we need to go to our menu manager and create a link to our SOBI2 component.

To create a link to our new component, carry out the steps below:

1. Create a link to the SOBI2 component and call it **Listings**. Go to **Menu |
   Main Menu | New SOBI2 | Latest entries**. SOBI2 provides us with various
   menu options. We will create a menu for visitors to our site to view listings ,
   as shown in the following screenshot:

2. Save, refresh, and let's view what we have on the front-end.
3. Notice that we have a new link. When we click on this link as a guest to the
   site, we will see the latest app review listings.

There are no apps listed at this time because we have not entered any. We have
configured the SOBI component and it is ready for use.

Listing apps

At this time, we have no listings and we have barely started our community. We have still not given people a reason to come to our site. Content is the key. Well, advertising is probably the best way to tell people about our site, but then if we do not have content, they will probably not return.

Let's list some apps:

1. Click on **Add Entry**.

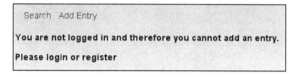

2. We, of course, cannot enter listings unless we are a registered member. So we need to click on **Sign up--Become a Reviewer**, and then log in, go to the listings menu to add an entry.

3. Complete the form and select all of the categories to which this app belongs. The form has been broken down into three parts as follows.

   ° PART 1: Enter the title, description, and the cost of the app.

Add New Entry

All fields with * are required.

Title *	Name of App
Description	**B** *I* U -- Font family -- -- Font size -- ABC ≡ ≡ ≡ ≡ ↺ ↻ HTML — ⊶ ⦂ ☰ ☷ Enter what it can do/ or what it does
Cost	Cost ✔ Free ☐ $0.99 ✔ $1.99 ☐ $2.99

- ° PART 2: Enter any additional information. We can also upload images for this app.

- ° PART 3: Select all of the categories associated with this app, and then click n **Send**.

4. Apps are set to be automatically published, so let's click on the listings link again to view the apps that we have listed.

5. Notice that there are now two listings, and they look pretty good, with an image. We should encourage our users to include images with their listings. Click on the title of the app to learn more about it.

Reviewing apps

Reviewing listed apps is intuitive. After we click on the title to learn more about the app, the view provides us with the opportunity to review the app. We do this by selecting how many stars that we want to attribute to the app, and then clicking on **Write Review**.

Rate now: 3

Want to write in a review?
Share your thoughts and experiences with this app.

Name: jlord_test_user100
Email: jlord_test_user100@gmail.com
Show my email ☑
Title: Music ID Review

Text:
```
this song. I had just got my Samsung Eternity
from AT&T and wanted to try out all the cool
features. I had the trial version to try out 7
Music Ids so I thought, Why Not.

Within a few seconds....literally a few seconds,
i had my song tile. It was totally cool.
Well, I used the trial version and did not want
to pay a hefty $0.99 cents each time I used it.
And, I did not want to pay $2.99 per month for
unlimited use either. So, I canceled the service.
```

Send

Reviews are published instantaneously. Click on the **Listings** menu to see the difference. Notice that the listings have stars.

Search   Add Entry
New Entries

MusicID

- $0.99
- $2.99

MobiVJ

- Free
Need to have high speed internet on your cell phone for this to work well.

When we click on the title, we will notice that in addition to the description of the app, the app reviews also appear on this page.

SOBI2 makes it very easy to add an app rating system to our site. Although the SOBI component is primarily designed to be a directory extension, a few plugin additions and code tweaks to the extension can turn it into an effective rating system.

> Another Joomla! review extension to consider is JReviews.
> JReviews can be purchased from the JReviews website (http://www.
> reviewsforjoomla.com/). Make sure that your host server supports
> the following requirements: **PHP5.2.x with json** and **mbstring extensions**,
> as well as **ionCube loaders**.

Displaying listings in profiles

The **SOBI2 Entries plugin** enables users to display their listings on their profile (plg_sobiposts-0.2.zip). This plugin, found on the JomSocial website (under Addons), permits us to integrate JomSocial and SOBI2. In *Chapter 2, JomSocial: Setup and Configuration*, we learned how to install JomSocial plugins, which then appear as applications in our profile. Let's install this plugin through the same process (from the back-end, install/uninstall).

Once installed, the plugin becomes one of the applications that users can add to their profile.

Users' app listings will then appear under their profile.

My Listings		
Title	**Category**	**Date Added**
MobiVJ	Apple, Music	March 14th, 2010

Notice that we gave users the option to make this app a part of their profile. Administrators can also make this a core application, in which case, it will be a part of everyone's profile.

Multimedia

A social networking site is not complete without the ability to share images and videos. Adding multimedia can be done from two places: under our **Profile**, and under the **Applications** menu, then **Photos** and **Videos**.

My Status

Share your thoughts here...

/ Edit profile   ⚙ Add applications   🔒 Write Message

🖼 Change profile picture   ⠿ Start a new group   ✉ View your inbox

🔒 Privacy   ✉ Invite Friends   ⊡ Upload photos

📹 Add Video

1. From your profile, click on **Upload photos**.

Upload multiple photos

All Photos | **My Photos**

No album created yet. Create one now

2. Enter the album information, and then click on **Create one now**.

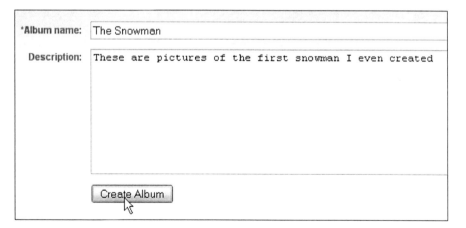

Album name: The Snowman

Description: These are pictures of the first snowman I even created

Create Album

Our network provides us with the opportunity to organize our images. We can create more than one album and upload more than one image at a time. The upload time depends on the size of the images and the server settings. You will see an image upload success message if the images have been uploaded successfully.

Home	Profile	Friends	Applications	Inbox

Upload multiple photos

Back to album | All Photos | My Photos

> Album images will be uploaded to

Select photo album

The Snowman ⌄ 📷 View Album

*You have uploaded **0** out of **500** allowed photo uploads.* ◄─

> Appheads are permitted to upload no more than 500 images in total

C:\Documents and Settings\Beatrice Bc [Browse...] ☐ Set as album cover

> As you add images, more windows will appear to upload more than one image at a time.

C:\Documents and Settings\Beatrice Bc [Browse...] ☐ Set as album cover

[Upload another photo] [Start Upload]

[Maximum upload file size **25** (MB)]

Let's click on **View Album** to view our virtual snowmen. We can also click on the images to see the full-size image.

These are pictures of the first snowman I even created

Videos

Uploading videos uses a similar process to photos. Within our network, we have two options for including videos. The first option is to upload videos to our own server. While this is great for allowing users to share their original videos, it could soon overload your server space. If you are like most of us and have shared hosting, you may want to be cautious about permitting your users to upload videos. This can be turned off in the administrative back-end.

The other option for including videos is through existing video websites, such as YouTube, Metacafe, and Google Videos. This option can minimize server overload issues, and should be encouraged for that reason. Besides, we are all going through an overload of information and passwords that are at multiple places. Having a way to consolidate resources and information is encouraged.

1. Go to **Applications | Videos**, and then click on **Add Video**, in order to open a window that will present you with two options: link, and upload.

    The window provides you with information on which providers or video websites can be used with the network, and provides the video specifications if we opt to upload our own video. Remember, the upload video option will not show if it is turned off by the administrator.

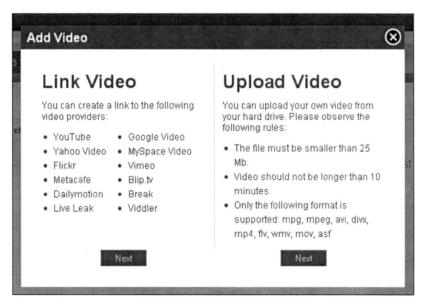

2. Adding a YouTube video: Click on **Next** under **Link Video**. Enter the URL of the video in the window that opens; select the category and to whom you want to show the video. The categories are set by the administrator. This website is about cell phone apps, so we found a video on YouTube on cell phone apps titled "My Top 10 Best iPhone Apps".

Link Video ⊗

> ***Video URL** [www.youtube.com/watch?v=A8SVrpiKKpQ]
>
> **Category** [General ▼]
>
> **Who can see** ◉ Public
> ○ Site Members
> ○ Friends
> ○ Only me
>
> *You have uploaded **0** out of **50** allowed video uploads.*
>
> **Link Video**

If the video is successfully linked, it will appear in the user's videos and in the networks activity stream. This may not always work if you are working locally (localhost).

My Videos

| All Videos | **My Videos** | Search |

> My Top 10 Best iPhone Apps
> 0 views
> Last updated: *less than a minute ago*
> Edit | Delete
>
> 07:36

3. Uploading videos: Click on **Next** under **Upload Video.** This process is similar to uploading images. The administrator can add file size restrictions to it.

Adding multimedia to our social network is easy and intuitive. Any user will be able to figure it out.

Summary

Our website is becoming exciting. Users can add content to our site; a few apps have been listed and reviewed, and there is some multimedia. Joomla! and JomSocial are fully extensible and allow integration with other Joomla! components. The system can work as-is, without any extensions. It mostly depends on the overall goal of your site. We will continue to build connections and create content in *Chapter 6, Community Building and Interaction* through group creation.

6
Community Building and Interaction

Online communication in the form of messages and information exchange on social networks has become a significant part of human communication. Social networks are facilitating inter-personal communication and the dissemination of all kinds of information and media content. As online messages and information exchange on social networks increase, more social networking sites have emerged around the world. Some of the notable ones are Nexopia (Canada), StudiVZ (Germany), iWiW (Hungary), Tuenti (Spain), Orkut, and Hi5 in South America and Central America. Other social network sites are Friendster, Gowalla, and Bebo. A good list of social networks is available on Wikipedia.org at: `http://en.wikipedia.org/wiki/List_of_social_networking_websites`.

There are social networking sites for almost every human activity. However, there are two broad categories of such networks: profit and non-profit social networks. Examples of profit sites are:

- Gurgle—a social networking site for parenting owned by Mothercare: `http://www.gurgle.com/default.aspx`

- QQ—an instant messaging service in China that also provides online games, pets, and ringtone downloads: `http://www.qq.com`

- Mixi—a site for meeting and interacting with people in Japan: `http://www.mixi.jp`

- Cyworld—a Korean site for friendship: `http://www.cyworld.com.cn/main`

- Yelp—a US product and services review site: `http://www.yelp.com`

The following are examples of non-profit sites geared toward social and development programs:

- SixDegrees.org: `http://www.sixdegrees.org`
- TakingITGlobal: `http://www.tigweb.org`
- Care2: `http://www.care2.com`
- Idealist.org: `http://www.idealist.org`
- WiserEarth: `http://www.wiserearth.org`
- OneWorldTV: `http://tv.oneworld.net`
- FreeRepublic: `http://www.freerepublic.com/home.htm`
- OneClimate: `http://www.oneclimate.net`
- Network for Good: `http://www1.networkforgood.org`

Online communities form and develop around specific interests and activities. For our site to be effective and valuable to its users, we need to determine the type of community that we want to build. Next, we need to decide what our community members will be able to do within the network: will they have a private messaging system, discussion forums, message boards, and can they share images and videos?

Our social networking system, JomSocial, allows users to create communities (known as groups within the system). An administrator of a JomSocial social networking site can set up how many groups (or communities) users can create. She or he can set the type of activities community members can perform and the limits of such activities. For instance, as administrators, we can decide whether members can upload videos and images, engage in group discussions, and post messages on walls. Also, administrators can determine the limits of user activities by deciding how many images and videos they can upload, and the number of discussion messages and wall messages users can post in a given time frame. We made some of these decisions as administrators in *Chapter 2, JomSocial: Setup and Configuration.*

In order for a social networking site to facilitate effective communication and user-regulated interaction, the site administrator will have to address the following concerns:

1. Is our community interface user-friendly and easy to navigate? This is essential because an interface that makes it easy to find things and makes interaction easy also attracts and keeps users.

2. How are we going to attract users to our community? Why would users want to join the community? Are there any benefits? These are some of the most challenging questions for any community. Communities exist because of people. Communities exist because of relationships and therefore, as a group or community owner and manager, we need to ensure that community members are continuously engaged and contribute to group activities.

3. How do we get members to take ownership of their community? Ownership is important. Each community probably needs a leader. Members must take responsibility for their community; they must nurture it and help it grow.

In this chapter, we will:

- Create groups or communities and let the groups appear in our profile
- Build and manage communities by:
    - Changing the community avatar
    - Creating group content
    - Attracting community members
    - Moderating communities
    - Encouraging members to contribute to group activities
    - Promoting the network to others
    - Reporting group activities to the administrator
    - Leaving the community
    - Removing group content

Creating communities or groups

We have previously created accounts, and added apps to our profiles. Our next task is to create communities or groups.

Create a community by carrying out the steps below:

1. Log in from the front-end. We will log in as Jackie Newperson. We can create a new group by going to **Applications | Groups | Create,** or by selecting **Start a New Group** from the menu below **My Status.**

2. Complete the form:

*Group name	App-xercise
*Description	Apps for working out. This group is for those using the apps for weight loss. Are the apps working our for you? Have you lost weight? What are some of the challenges you have come across? Are there any tips you would like to share with us
*Category	iphone
Group type	● Open Anyone can join and view this group. ○ Private This group requires approval for new members to join. Anyone can view the group's description. Only group members content.

We can select a **Category**. Available categories are pre-defined by the administrator; we set them up in *Chapter 2, JomSocial: Setup and Configuration.*

We can make our groups open or private.

Discussion ordering	● Order by last replied ○ Order by creation date
Photos	○ Disable group photos. ● Allow members to upload photos and create albums ○ Allow only group admins to upload photos and create albums.
Group Albums	6
Videos	○ Disable group videos. ● Allow members to upload videos. ○ Allow only group admins to upload videos.
Group Videos	6

Fields marked with an asterisk (*) are required.

[Create Group] [Cancel]

3. Complete the settings, and then click on **Create Group**.

4. Click on **View your group now** to preview our first community.

At this point, our community is new. We have our own menu, we can edit our avatar (group image), and we can share announcements, have discussions, share pictures and videos, and post messages on our wall. We can also modify the group settings by clicking on **Edit** and changing some of the settings that we made during the community creation process.

Showing your groups under your profile

Users' groups appear under their profile. We did this in *Chapter 3, Remote Installation and Managing User Profiles* when we added applications to our profile, including the group application. To ensure that the group application is activated, we will have to do the following:

1. Log in as a user (Jackie NewPerson).

2. Go to **Applications | My applications** in order to view all of the applications made available to users by the administrator. The group application should appear in this list.

3. If the group application does not appear in the list of available applications, click on **Browse**, find the group application, and add it.

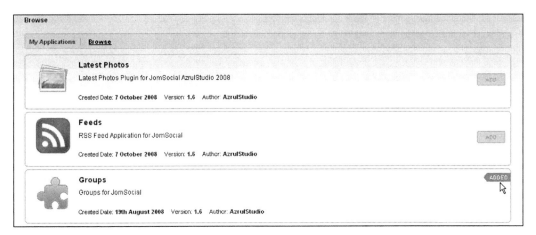

4. Go back to our profile by clicking on **Profile**. The groups we belong to now appear in our profile.

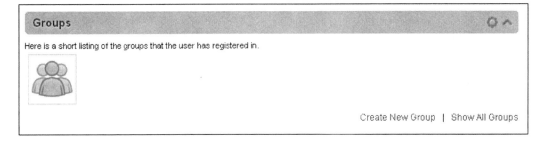

The location of each application is dependent upon the administrator settings. As an administrator, we may want to move the group application to a location that is more visible. This can be done from the administrative back-end. As an administrator, the group extension is one of the applications that we may want to consider as one of the core applications. If we do not make it a core application, not every user will be able to activate this application by adding it to his or her application. We may want to notify users of the existence of such applications if we do not make it a core application.

We have created a group; we need to make it attractive for others to participate in the group. We will log in as a user and create two more groups: Google Nexus apps for music and iPhone apps for music.

Building and managing our community

Building a community starts with the owner of the community. How do we make it attractive enough to get others involved? We created three communities, each with a unique niche. How then do we encourage other users to join our community? We provided a community description when we created our site. Now we need to give our community a character.

Advertising communities

By default, groups appear on the front page of JomSocial (if they are set to appear). The administrator can go through the JomSocial configuration process, deciding how many groups should appear on the JomSocial front page. (For more information, please refer to *Chapter 2, JomSocial: Setup and Configuration*.) This is done from the back-end by clicking on **Components | JomSocial | Configuration | Layout**. The settings can be changed under **Frontpage**, as shown in the following screenshot.

Frontpage		
Frontpage activities	10	
Frontpage recent members	30	Users
Frontpage recent videos	5	Videos
Frontpage recent photos	3	Photos
Frontpage recent groups	5	Groups
Show search	Hide	
Show who's online	Members Only	
Show latest members	Show	
Show activity stream	Show	
Show latest videos	Show	
Show latest groups	Show	
Show latest photos	Show	

Take note of the Activity Stream. Enabling this feature and making it show on the front page will stream all individual and group activities on the main JomSocial page. This is another way to inform visitors about what is happening on the site, at a glance.

After we log out and go back to the main network page (click on **Sign Up--Become a Reviewer**), notice that the groups appear on the main page, as shown in the following screenshot.

Click on **View all Groups** to see all of the groups (or communities) that have been created.

Changing a community avatar

Do the following to change a community avatar:

1. Log in from the front-end (as the owner of a group). We will log in as Jackie NewPerson, the creator of the App-xercise community.

2. Click on **Applications | Groups**, and then click on the community title.

3. From the group site, click on **Edit Avatar**. The process is similar to the way in which we uploaded individual avatars. Click on **Browse** to locate the group image, and then click on **Upload** in order to update the avatar with the new image.

App-xercise	**Group Information (You are the group owner)**
	Category: iPhone
	Name: App-xercise
	Description: Apps for working out. This group is for those
	Have you lost weight? What are some of the
	share with us
	Created: Friday, 26 March 2010
	Creator: Jackie NewPerson

4. Our community now has an attractive avatar. What a great way to promote our group!

Earlier in this chapter, we mentioned some concerns that we need to address when building communities. These included the need to attract users to our network. Our next task is to create some content and invite others to join our community.

Creating group content

1. We are still logged in as Jackie NewPerson, the creator of the App-xercise community.

Each group has the ability to create announcements (or bulletins/news), start and contribute to discussions, share pictures, share videos, and post comments on the group wall.

2. Click on **Create Bulletin**. Complete the form, and then click on **Add News**.

3. Click on **Create Discussion**. Complete the form, and then click on **Add Discussion**.

4. The processes for creating a group album and uploading pictures and videos are similar to what individuals do to their profile. This was discussed in the previous chapter ; we can follow the same processes to create the group album.

5. The group wall is self-explanatory. It is similar to having a group discussion.

For our information, our activities appear on the group page, as shown in the screenshot below:

Remember: a group is only as good as its activities and content, and the members that contribute to the group interaction. We have created some content, as the owner of the App-xercise group. We need to attract other users so that they can contribute to the group's activities.

Attracting community members

Our website, Kifari.com, is a site for app reviews and ratings. It is an open community and users need to be registered to contribute, rate, and review apps. In Chapters 3, 4, and 5, we created profiles, made connections with other users, and created some content. We all belong to the main Kifari community.

Our social network's group function permits us to create our own niches within Kifari.com. We have created some communities, and now we need to share information about our community and attract users. There are two options for bringing users into our community. We can invite our friends, or users can self-invite (users invite themselves to the group).

Option 1: Inviting our friends

1. Invite friends by clicking on the **Invite Friends** tab:

2. Select the friends that you want to invite, write a brief message, and then click on **Submit**. Jackie has two friends—test users 113 and 87. We invited both of them; invitations are sent to the users' e-mail addresses associated with their registration. The e-mail will contain information on how to accept or reject invitation.

JomSocial uses the **Cronjob/Scheduled Task Process** to send e-mails. This needs to be activated in the Administrative back-end in order for the JomSocial system to be able to deliver invitations to invitees' e-mail inboxes. To do that, log in to the back-end, and then go to **Components | JomSocial | Configurations**. The cron jobs feature is under the **Site** tab. Select **Yes**, and then click on **Save**.

Option 2: Inviting yourself to join a group

Groups appear on the main page of our social network; to invite yourself, perform these tasks:

1. Click on **Home** on the main profile page, and then click on **View all groups**.

2. Click on the title of a group (we clicked on **iPhone Apps for Music**). This opens the group's page. Click on **Join Group** to join the group.

3. Click on **Yes** to join the group. Notice that there are now two appheads in the **iPhone apps for music** community.

If the group is a private group, you will receive a message that the owner of the group has been notified, and the owner will have to approve the request before you can become a group member.

Moderating communities

Moderation settings are dependent upon the administrator. When we set up our social network in *Chapter 2, JomSocial: Setup and Configuration*, we decided that group creation does not need administrator approval. That is one level of moderation.

The second level of moderation occurs at the community level. Group owners can moderate group activities by deciding whether members can post activities and how many posts, videos, and images members can add or post. This is done by clicking on the **Edit** button which is (visible only to group owners).

Once you become a member of a community, you are ready to contribute to it. The owner of the group may have already created some content, and community members will need to contribute in order to ensure that the group grows.

Group members can participate in discussions, contribute videos and images, and post comments on the group wall. The Bulletins and announcements are reserved for the group owner.

There are other group activity plugins (available at `http://www.socialcode.co.uk`) that can be used to enhance group activities, for instance, group URL and group file sharing. These are usually in the form of plugins like the following:

- **JS Activity Comments**: Allows users to comment on the activity stream
- **Custom Group URLs**: Allows groups to have custom URLs
- **JomSocial File sharing**: Allows file sharing within JomSocial communities

Promoting the network

The best way to get more people to be a part of a community is to advertise the community to non-users or your friends using other systems. The **Share this** tool enables us to share our group with our friends who are not yet a part of this network.

We can share our network with our friends on other popular social networks or we can send information directly to our friends' e-mail. Again, we need to remember that the cron jobs feature needs to be enabled in the back-end in order for this to work.

Share this

Share this via link:

Facebook	del.icio.us	Digg
Windows Live	Stumbleupon	Furl
Blinklist	G Bookmarks	Diigo
My Space	Twitter	Xanga
Bebo	Twine	Blogmarks
Faves	AIM	Technorati
LinkedIn	Y! Bookmarks	Newsvine

Or Send to email:

Enter email addresses; separate multiple recipients with commas.

Message: (Optional)

Share this page   **Cancel**

Reporting group activities to the administrator

Although we hope that all groups will have user-friendly activities, some activities may need reporting. Users can report a group by simply clicking on the **Report group** link, completing the form, and submitting the form to the administrator.

Report group   Share this

Delete Group   Edit   Edit Avatar

The settings of this tool are set by the administrator and are done through the JomSocial configuration process. The settings can always be changed or modified.

Leaving the community

We all want to be part of bustling dynamic communities. However, group members have the option to leave a group if they lose interest or decide not to continue to be a part of the group. The **Leave Group** option appears on group members' accounts, providing an easy way of leaving a group. We can leave any time, no questions asked!

Group owners also have the option to disband or delete the group. This option is available only to group owners. Clicking on **Delete Group** will remove a group from the social networking system.

Removing group content

Only group owners can remove entire group posts. This can be done by clicking on the **Edit** button.

This menu also allows us to make changes to our group. The group's content and activities can be removed or reset by selecting the checkbox next to **Remove associated activities**, and then clicking on **Save**.

Remove associated ☑
activities   By checking this option, all existing activities that are associated with this group will be removed

Fields marked with an asterisk (*) are required.

Save   Cancel

Summary

The interactions that we have had indicate that the interface of our community is simple and that the features are easy to find and use. As we continued to test our site in the online environment, we have gained confidence that our social network site is user-friendly enough for others to use. We may test it by having others use the system to determine its ease of use.

As we recall, all activities are logged on the main page of our network. We can always go there to see what our users have been up to.

Building communities is one of the basic applications that facilitate user interaction. In addition to becoming friends with other users, having a community of individuals who share similar interests is a good way of promoting interactions in a social network.

The interface is simple, intuitive, and the features of the system are easy to find. Learning how everything works takes time. In this chapter, we created and managed our communities. In the next chapter, we will get into some technical details of how to customize our template.

7
Customizing the JomSocial Template

The main objective of a service-oriented site is to understand the context in which the information on the site will be delivered, and the kind of audience it is for. Contextually, our site will have most of its content generated by the visitors who are expected to post content on the site, and also use content posted by others in order to enhance their mobile phone use. To this end, a good knowledge of the kind of users and visitors that we expect on our website is crucial to the site's success.

The layout and services provided on the site need to take into consideration the four elements of human communication identified by Bordewijk and van Kaam (*Towards a New Classification of Tele-Information Services* in *The New Media Reader*, Wardrip-Fruin, N and Montfort N (Eds) 2003 published by the MIT Press, Cambridge and London) classified information traffic patterns of electronic networks: allocution, conversation, consultation, and registration.

- Allocution: Refers to traffic pattern, where a networked service facilitates the storage of information that is then delivered to users of the network
- Conversation: Is the interactivity that is made possible through an electronic system that allows the exchange of information between users
- Consultation: Is the communication pattern that takes place within an electronic system that permits the delivery of information upon a request from a user
- Registration: Refers to the communication pattern within an electronic system that allows the gathering of information from users; this could be user-generated content

A social networking site as an electronic communication system has the potential to seamlessly integrate all four forms of human electronic communication patterns when carefully planned and implemented. Our main goal in this chapter is to lay out the front page and the user menus so that they can incorporate the four patterns of communication. This will facilitate the desired level of interactivity among the potential users of the site. To do this, we need to make sure that our layout ensures that the user login link and links to site content are prominently displayed on the site for easy use. The main focus is to ensure that, regardless of the kind of layout we choose for our site, access to the site login, links to site content, and user menus should be situated on the site such that users will not have difficulty in finding them.

Laying out our site is a form of branding that requires the customization of the site's look. To customize our site, we will have to tinker with the site's template. Most of us may not know how to design a template; we probably rely on other talents to create the template that we use. We adopted the Quasar template from RocketTheme for our Joomla! installation. It has a GPL license, and works with minimal customization. Also, our installed JomSocial component has a template that integrates with any Joomal! template. However, we will need to make some JomSocial template customization in order to ensure that our site has a user interface that is efficiently interactive and provides the service that we set out to offer to our potential users.

In this chapter, we will customize the JomSocial template by doing the following:

- Duplicating the default template and changing some of its elements
- Changing the default avatars of the template for individuals and groups
- Changing the background color of the template
- Creating a new set of user menus

Duplicating the JomSocial template

Start the customization process by duplicating the default template folder and renaming it. The default folder will be renamed **kifari** and the duplicate will be called **default**.

1. Duplicate the default template folder by going to our site's root folder: `components\com_community\template` folder, and then right click and copy, then paste, and then rename the folder.
2. Rename the default template to use a unique name, we named ours kifari, and the duplicate will be called default.

3. Next, log into the Joomla! administrative back-end and then go to the JomSocial component: **Components | JomSocial | Configurations | Layout**. The templates are under template settings. Notice that the kifari template is now available as an option. Select it, and then save your selection.

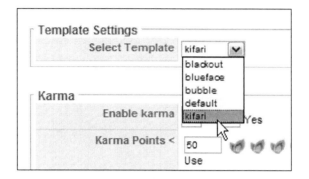

We have now changed the name of the default template, after duplicating it. The default template is now named kifari, and we will continue the customization and template modification using this template.

Changing the avatars for individuals and groups

We are about to change the default images, in order to make them our own. Some of the default images can be found in the following directory: `rootfolder/ components/com_comunity/assets/`. This directory can be accessed through your FTP client or the root folder of your site through your hosting cpanel.

We will change the default avatar and thumbnails for groups and individuals, by modifying the following images: `default.jpg`, `default_thumb.jpg`, `group.jpg`, and `group_thumb.jpg`.

To change the avatars, carry out the steps shown below:

1. Locate the following files: `default.jpg`, `default_thumb.jpg`, `group.jpg`, and `group_thumb.jpg` in the template directory.

2. Determine the images dimensions and sizes.

3. Create our own default images using photo editing software. Keep the same image names.

4. Upload the new images to the images directory. We have to make sure that we are overwriting the old files with new ones that have the same names.

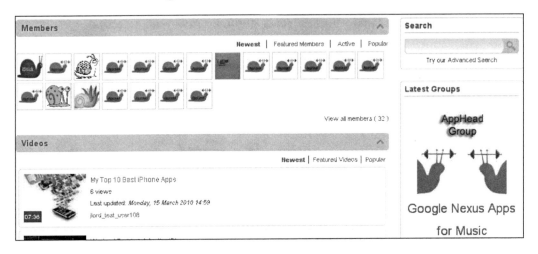

Notice that the default profile and individual images have been updated with our new images. We may change the other images in this folder to further customize the look of the template.

Changing the background color of the template

If we intend to keep the site simple but efficient, the JomSocial default template is great. A plain white or plain color background is always attractive. We may want to remove the classic JomSocial green and sand colors. These changes can be made in the same folder as the default and thumbnail images. In order to keep the design measurements consistent, we will have to keep the same dimensions.

- The image files can be located in the template images folder: `components\com_community\templates\default\images\` (or replace `default` with your template name)

- The images we may want to look at are:
  `toolbar.png`
  `app-box-header.png`

- Other files can be found in the toolbar sub-directory:
  `toolbar-bg.gif`
  `toolbar-item-on-left.gif`
  `toolbar-item-on-right.gif`

The CSS file can be found in the css folder. A good CSS editor will also show us how the changes that we are making will affect the template, before making your changes. Some good CSS editors are Dreamweaver, Expression Web (formerly Frontpage), and KompoZer (http://www.kompozer.net/). KompoZer is an open source web authoring tool.

Modifying the JomSocial main page

We will change the text on the front page, as well as the **JOIN US NOW, IT'S FREE** button.

To modify this part of the template requires two steps: identifying the code, and modifying it.

Identifying the code

Open the kifari template folder, locate the frontpage.guests.php file, and open it (in a web design editor that you may have, for example Dreamweaver or, Expression Web, KompoZer, or Nvu). Now let's examine the file:

- The top part of almost all PHP files will have some copyright information. Note that the company that developed JomSocial permits template modification and creation. The asterisk indicates that these lines are not a part of the code that affects the execution of the page; they are comments.

```php
<?php
/**
 * @package         JomSocial
 * @subpackage      Template
 * @copyright (C) 2008 by Slashes & Dots Sdn Bhd - All rights
 reserved!
```

```
 * @license http://www.jomsocial.com Copyrighted Commercial
Software
 *
 */
defined('_JEXEC') or die();
?>
<div class="greybox">
    <div>
        <div>
        <table cellpadding="0" cellspacing="0" border="0" width="100%">
                <tr>
```

- The part starting at `defined('_JEXEC') or die();` is the beginning of the code that affects the execution of the page. `<table cellpadding="0" cellspacing="0" border="0" width="100%">` is the opening code of a table. The part that we want to edit in the image from the previous page is available in a table with one row and two columns.

Left column

Let's take a look at the components of the left column.

Get connected

The left column of the JomSocial template is written by the following code:

```
<td valign="top">
<div class="introduction">
<h1><?php echo JText::_('CC GET CONNECTED TITLE'); ?></h1>
```

The above code represents **Get Connected!**, as shown on the front page of the JomSocial template.

The following code defines the bulleted points on the front page as given below:

- Connect and expand your network
- View profiles and add new friends
- Share your photos and videos
- Create your own group or join others

```
        <ul id="featurelist">
         <li><?php echo JText::_('CC CONNECT AND EXPAND'); ?></li>
          <li><?php echo JText::_('CC VIEW PROFILES AND ADD
            FRIEND'); ?></li>
```

```
<li><?php echo JText::_('CC SHARE PHOTOS AND VIDEOS');
    ?></li>
<li><?php echo JText::_('CC CREATE OWN GROUP OR JOIN');
    ?></li>
</ul>
```

Removing a bullet

If we want only three lines, we need to remove one bulleted list.

```
ul id="featurelist">
    <li><?php echo JText::_('CC CONNECT AND EXPAND'); ?></li>
    <li><?php echo JText::_('CC VIEW PROFILES AND ADD FRIEND');
        ?></li>
    <li><?php echo JText::_('CC SHARE PHOTOS AND VIDEOS');
        ?></li>
</ul>
```

Note that in order to remove a bulleted point, we will have to remove a complete line of code, for instance, `<li><?php echo JText::_('CC CREATE OWN GROUP OR JOIN'); ?></li>`. We have to take out the `<li></li>` tags and everything in between. If some code is left, the template may no longer work. After removing the code, save the file in its original folder, refresh your page, and enjoy it.

Modifying the code

We have identified where we can change the **Get Connected!** text. Our website is about app reviews. Let's change **Get Connected!** to **Become an Apphead!**.

1. Find and open the en-GB.com_community.ini file. This file can be found at root folder/language/en-GB/en-GB.com_community.ini. Open the file in a web editor. When opened in Notepad, it will look jumbled and almost impossible to decipher.

2. Go through the lines and locate the line CC GET CONNECTED TITLE. The search and replace function in your code editor can help you to locate this line.

```
718
719 ⊟ CC GET CONNECTED TITLE=Get Connected!
720   CC CONNECT AND EXPAND=Connect and expand your network
721   CC BUTTON LOGIN=Login
722   CC BUTTON CLOSE=Close
723   CC PHOTO ALBUM BY=By
```

3. When you find the line, you will see: CC GET CONNECTED TITLE=Get Connected!. Change the information after the equal sign from **Get Connected!** to **Become an Apphead!**. The new code will read: CC GET CONNECTED TITLE=Become an Apphead!

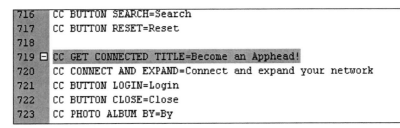

```
716   CC BUTTON SEARCH=Search
717   CC BUTTON RESET=Reset
718
719 ⊟ CC GET CONNECTED TITLE=Become an Apphead!
720   CC CONNECT AND EXPAND=Connect and expand your network
721   CC BUTTON LOGIN=Login
722   CC BUTTON CLOSE=Close
723   CC PHOTO ALBUM BY=By
```

4. Save the en-GB.com_community.ini file and upload it. Refresh your page, and *voila!* We are now inviting people to be appheads! We will have to repeat this process to change the other bulleted text.We intend to have only two bulleted points, and will also change the text on the join button.

5. Change of the four bullets to two with the following text:

   - List, review, and recommend apps
   - Share app experiences

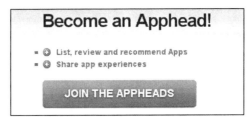

Notice the change in text and the number of bulleted points on the front page.

Adding a bullet point

To add a bullet point, copy a complete line of code—everything between an `<li>` and an `</li>`—for an existing bullet point, for example:

```
<li><?php echo JText::_('CC SHARE PHOTOS AND VIDEOS'); ?></li>
```

and change the text of the bullet to the desired text. In our case, we changed it as follows:

```
<li><?php echo JText::_('Learn about mobile phone apps'); ?></li>
```

> We changed the text by using a sentence format (not in all capitals) and deleted the "CC" because we do not need to change the code in the en-GB.com_community.ini file.

The code in the `frontpage.guests.php` file should now look like this:

```
ul id="featurelist">
        <li><?php echo JText::_('CC CONNECT AND EXPAND'); ?></li>
        <li><?php echo JText::_('CC VEW PROFILES AND ADD FRIEND');
            ?></li>
        <li><?php echo JText::_('CC SHARE PHOTOS AND VIDEOS'); ?></li>
<li><?php echo JText::_('Learn about mobile phone apps'); ?></li>
    </ul>
```

Save the file (`frontpage.guests.php`), upload it into the kifari template folder, refresh the site, and notice the changed list of bullets.

- ⊗ List, review and recommend apps
- ⊗ Share app experiences
- ⊗ Learn about mobile phone apps

The Join button

The text **JOIN NOW IT'S FREE!** over a green button is rendered by the code below:

```
<div class="joinbutton">
        <a id="joinButton" href="<?php echo CRoute::_(index.
php?option=com_community&view=register', false ); ?>" title="<?php
echo JText::_('CC JOIN US NOW'); ?>">
        <?php echo JText::_('CC JOIN US NOW'); ?> </a>
```

In lay terms, any code that begins with CC, or any other code that begins with JText::_(" (for example:'CC GET CONNECTED TITLE') represents a changeable value that can be found in the Language folder in the main Joomla! installation root folder file (joomla installation root folder/language/en-GB: en-GB.com_community.ini).

> We do not need to alter most of the code found in the frontpage.guests.php file. The required alteration will be made in the en-GB.com_community.ini file.

Right-hand column

The right-hand column on the JomSocial template is generated by the
following code:

```
<td width="200">
        <div class="loginform">
<form action="<?php echo CRoute::getURI();?>" method="post"
name="login" id="form-login" >
<h2><?php echo JText::_('CC MEMBER LOGIN'); ?></h2>
     <label>
<?php echo JText::_('CC USERNAME'); ?><br />
<input type="text" class="inputbox frontlogin" name="username"
id="username" />
  </label>
<label>
        <?php echo JText::_('CC PASSWORD'); ?><br />
        <input type="password" class="inputbox frontlogin"
name="passwd" id="password" />
                      </label>
        <?php if(JPluginHelper::isEnabled('system',
            'remember')) : ?>
                      <label for="remember">
   <input type="checkbox" alt="<?php echo JText::_('CC REMEMBER MY
DETAILS'); ?>" value="yes" id="remember" name="remember"/>
   <?php echo JText::_('CC REMEMBER MY DETAILS'); ?>
                      </label>
                      <?php endif; ?>

                      <div style="text-align: center;
                        padding: 10px 0 5px;">
                      <input type="submit" value="<?php echo
JText::_('CC BUTTON LOGIN');?>" name="submit" id="submit"
class="button" />
   <input type="hidden" name="option" value="com_user" />
   <input type="hidden" name="task" value="login" />
   <input type="hidden" name="return" value="<?php echo $return;
?>" />
                      <?php echo JHTML::_( 'form.token' ); ?>
                      </div>

                      <span>
                         <?php echo JText::_('CC FORGOT
YOUR'); ?> <a href="<?php echo CRoute::_( 'index.php?option=com_
user&view=reset' ); ?>" class="login-forgot-password"><span><?php
```

```
echo JText::_('CC PASSWORD'); ?></span></a> /
                              <a href="<?php echo CRoute::_( 'index.
php?option=com_user&view=remind' ); ?>" class="login-forgot-
username"><span><?php echo JText::_('CC USERNAME'); ?></span></a>?
                    </span>
                    <br />
                     <a href="<?php echo CRoute::_( 'index.
php?option=com_community&view=register&task=activation' ); ?>"
class="login-forgot-username">
                          <span><?php echo JText::_('CC RESEND
ACTIVATION CODE'); ?></span>
                      </a>
                    </form>
                    <?php echo $fbHtml;?>
                </div>
              </td>
            </tr>
          </table>
```

This is the login form where we enter our username and password.

Creating a new menu link in the JomSocial toolbar

JomSocial allows the modification of its toolbar. Instead of having separate Joomla! links on our website for listing and reviewing apps, we can create a new menu within the JomSocial profile toolbar that will serve this function.

The menu will be linked to the SOBI2 component that we installed in *Chapter 5, Creating Content and Sharing Activities*. We want our users to be able to list and review apps from their social network toolbar. We will name these menus: **List Apps** and **Recommend Apps**. They will be submenus (children) of the menu (parent) **To do list**.

Creating a new menu link is a two-step process:

Step 1: Identifying the file and adding the menu

1. First, identify where we want to put the new menu on the JomSocial toolbar. We will place our new menu between **Applications** and **Inbox**.

2. Identify the file that needs to be modified (`toolbar.index.php`, which is located in the directory with the following path: `components/com_ community/templates/your template`) and open it in a web editor. Identify the code at about line 122.

```
110        <li id="toolbar-item-apps" class="<?php echo $toolbarClass[TOOLBAR_APP];?>">
111            <a href="<?php echo $appItem->link; ?>" onmouseover="joms.toolbar.open('m
112                <?php echo $appItem->caption; ?>
113            </a>
114            <div id="m3" onmouseover="joms.toolbar.cancelclosetime()" onmouseout="jom
115                <?php echo $customToolbar->getMenuItems(TOOLBAR_APP, 'prepend'); ?>
116                <?php echo $customToolbar->getMenuItems(TOOLBAR_APP, 'append'); ?>
117            </div>
118        </li>
119    <?php
120            }
121        }
122    ?>
123
```

The new menu code will have to be inserted after `?>`

3. Enter the following code into the file:

```
<li class="" id="toolbar-item-apps">

<a onmouseout="joms.toolbar.closetime()" onmouseover="joms.
toolbar.open('m5')" href="/index.php?option=com_community&amp;v
iew=apps&amp;Itemid=2">To do list</a>

<div style="overflow: hidden; visibility: hidden;"
onmouseout="joms.toolbar.closetime()" onmouseover="joms.
toolbar.cancelclosetime()" id="m5">

<a ref="/index.php?option=com_community&amp;view=groups&amp;tas
k=mygroups&amp;userid=62&amp;Itemid=2">Item A</a>

<a href="/index.php?option=com_community&amp;view=photos&amp;ta
sk=myphotos&amp;userid=62&amp;Itemid=2">Item B</a>

<a href="/index.php?option=com_community&amp;view=videos&amp;ta
sk=myvideos&amp;userid=62&amp;Itemid=2">Item C</a>
</div>
</li>
```

Let us explain the links. The code between `<a ref="/` and `</a>` represents the URL that we want to link to. In this example, we duplicated the links from groups, photos, and videos under the **Applications** menu.

Save and upload the modified file, and then preview it.

We now have a new menu item called **To do list**. Our links are not yet functional; we still need to create meaningful links.

Before we do that, let's go through the code and understand what we did and how it affects the menu tabs.

- This top part creates a list beginning with the code `<li`:

```
<li class="" id="toolbar-item-apps">
<a onmouseout="joms.toolbar.closetime()" onmouseover="joms.
toolbar.open('m5')" href="/index.php?option=com_community&amp;v
iew=apps&amp;Itemid=2">To do list</a>
```

Notice that the menu is called `To do list`. We can change that to any title, by changing the title in the last line of the previous code.

```
href="/index.php?option=com_community&amp;view=apps&amp;Itemid=
2">To do list</a>
```

- The next code is for styling. We suggest you leave it as is:

```
<div style="overflow: hidden; visibility: hidden;"
onmouseout="joms.toolbar.closetime()" onmouseover="joms.toolbar.
cancelclosetime()" id="m5">
```

We can add more menus by copying and pasting the same code, but we will have to change the menu ID, which is identified in the example above as `m5`. Any additional menu will require a unique ID.

- The rest of the code is for submenu items:

```
<a href="/index.php?option=com_community&amp;view=apps&amp;Item
id=2">Item A</a>
```

Each line of code that begins with `<a href=" "` defines the actual link that we need to, link to and `">Item A</a` is the name (text) of the submenu. We will have to change this text if we want to change the name of the menu item.

`<a class="has-separator"` is a separator that is used to create an extra space between two submenus.

Our new menu has three submenus. If we wanted to delete some, or add or rearrange the existing ones, we need to adjust a submenu item between the following tags `<a>` `</a>`, that is:

```
href="/index.php?option=com_community&amp;view=apps&amp;task=brows
e&amp;Itemid=2">name of link</a>
```

Every open tag in the code, for instance `<li>`, needs a closing tag: `</li>`. This closes the list that we started. This is important, as the menu may not appear if the list tag is not closed.

Step 2: Making the new items linkable

1. We will first go back to the code that we previously inserted, and rename some of the submenu items, and delete others. We need one item (list apps). Note our changes in the code:

```
<li class="" id="toolbar-item-apps">
<a onmouseout="joms.toolbar.closetime()" onmouseover="joms.
toolbar.open('m5')" href="/index.php?option=com_community&amp;v
iew=apps&amp;Itemid=2">To do list</a>
<div style="overflow: hidden; visibility: hidden;"
onmouseout="joms.toolbar.closetime()" onmouseover="joms.
toolbar.cancelclosetime()" id="m5">
<a class="has-separator" href="/index.php?option=com_community&
amp;view=apps&amp;Itemid=2">List Apps</a>
</div> </li>
```

Our modified menu now appears as follows:

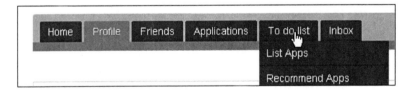

2. Go back to the code, and identify the code associated with the submenu item:

```
http://www.your web site.com/index.php?option=com_sobi2&sobi2Ta
sk=showNew&Itemid=10
```

Replace the code between `<a ref="/` and `</a>` with the previous code.

If you are creating a link to an application, or a link within the JomSocial component, then paste the code beginning with `index.php?option=com_sobi2&sobi2Task=showNew&Itemid=10`

However, if you are linking to another Joomal! extension, copy and paste the entire URL; for instance:

`http://www.your web site.com/index.php?option=com_sobi2&sobi2Task=showNew&Itemid=10`

3. Save and upload the page, refresh the website, and then test the link.

Simple template enhancements like this can improve the overall efficiency of our site. We can remove the submit listing from the main Joomla link and make it a part of the user menu (to be seen only by registered members).

 More information about template customization can be found on the JomSocial website at `http://www.jomsocial.com`.

Summary

Customizing or creating a template needs more than one chapter. We have attempted to provide some guidance on changing some of the features of your network with minimal developer experience. By making some changes to the default JomSocial template, we have made an attempt to customize the look of our site. Now that we know how to change some of the elements of our template and create a new set of user menu, we are now in the position to explore further customization of our JomSocial template. In the next chapter, we will explore other tips to finalize the overall look of our site.

8
Tips and Tricks

Throughout this book, we have focused largely on getting the social network operational. JomSocial works right out of the box with minimal configuration. In this chapter, we will finalize the look of the site and get it ready for use. We know our social network works, we know how to invite friends, and we have started work on the JomSocial template.

We need to plan the final look of our site before we start developing it. Know what you want and need. Some readers may already have functional sites and just need to add the social networking component to their site. So the first seven chapters may have provided all that you needed to get your social network up and running. As we finalize the look of our site, we will share some tips and tricks (hacks) that could enhance the overall experience of the users of our site.

Cursory looks at all of the social networks that we have identified in this book have indicated that the user interface of an online network is important to the success of the network. This is true for all online services: the user interface has to be user friendly and functional.

The JomSocial user interface is quite functional, but our challenge is to customize it for the service that we are offering online, by integrating it with the Joomla! content management system, the JReviews component, and about 18 plugins that we currently have on our site. In doing this, we have to use the following pointers as guides:

- For the visitors to our site, the user interface is the service; if the interface is difficult to navigate, then it will be difficult for visitors to use the service. Visitors to the site need to be able to browse around and perform their activities on the site with little or no hassle. The user interface has to be intuitive. This will ensure that visitors will use the service and be satisfied with it. Please refer to *User Interface Design Tips, Techniques, and Principles* at `http://www.ambysoft.com/essays/userInterfaceDesign.html`.

- We need to ensure that the user interface of our site is simple and facilitates efficient interaction. However, we have to understand that our site is dynamic and we will have to make incremental changes to meet the needs of the users. (For more information on user interface design, visit http://en.wikipedia.org/wiki/User_interface_design.)

In this chapter, we will discuss various tricks that we can use to simplify the user interface of our site for effective interaction. We will also identify some of the code hacks that we can make in order to ensure that our site is adaptable to the users' needs. We will accomplish this by doing the following:

- Making use of the JomSocial profile's positions
- Integrating JomSocial with other social networks: Facebook and Twitter
- Adding other items to the HelloMe module
- Moving installed apps above the activity stream
- Activating Joomla! SEF (Search Engine Friendly) links
- Modifying the PHP.ini file

Using the JomSocial profile's positions

The JomSocial profile template has various positions that can be used to further customize the look of the social network. JomSocial 1.8 has 10 module positions that allow us to add features to our social network:

- The module positions vary depending on the page you are on:
  - **js_side_top**: Appears before any content in the side column of the front page
  - **js_side_bottom**: Appears after any content in the side column of the front page

- The following six positions are available on individual profile pages:

  ○ **js_profile_top**: Placed between the toolbar and the profile page

  ○ **js_profile_bottom**: Placed after the profile page

  ○ **js_profile_side_top**: Placed before content in the side column of profile page, after **js_side_top**

  ○ **js_profile_side_bottom**: Placed after content in the side column of the profile page, before **js_side_bottom**

  ○ **js_profile_feed_top**: Placed before the activity stream section of the profile page

  ○ **js_profile_feed_bottom**: Placed after the activity stream section of the profile page

- The following two positions are available on individual profile pages:
  - **js_groups_side_top**: Placed before content in the side column of the groups page, after **js_side_top**
  - **js_groups_side_bottom**: Placed after content in the side column of the groups page, before **js_side_bottom**

We added some tools by installing SOBI2, and created the **Listings & Reviews** link (refer to *Chapter 5, Creating Content and Sharing Activities*). Our goal is to make the **mod_sobi2latest** module a part of our profile, so that the latest listings will also be displayed on the right-hand side of user profiles when users log in to the site.

Assigning modules to JomSocial module positions is similar to how it is done in Joomla!. The difference is that instead of selecting a module position, you have to type it in.

To position the **mod_sobi2latest** module, log in to the Joomla! administrator back-end and:

1. Click on the **Extensions | Module manager**.

2. Find an existing module (or create a module by using the custom option). We will duplicate the latest listings module to appear in the profiles, and then save our changes. The module will be placed in the **js_profile_side_top** position.

Very important: Make sure that you set the module to appear on all menus. If not, the module will not appear in the selected position.

3. Save the changes, refresh, and view the site.

Note that the latest listings now appear in the module position specified.

The features that appear in JomSocial module positions become permanent fixtures on user profiles. This could be a great way for the website administrator or owner to periodically advertise or showcase specific website features. Most Joomla! modules can be published in JomSocial positions.

Integrating other social networks

Facebook and Twitter have become synonymous with social networking. Having a Twitter or Facebook account can increase the visibility of our site and could encourage friends of our friends — and their friends — to visit our site.

JomSocial enables us to integrate Facebook and Twitter. With Facebook integration, users can connect to our site and import their Facebook information into their JomSocial profile in order to create an account. Twitter integration enables our users to show their tweets on their profile, and allows the site administrator (the owners of the site) to also show their tweets.

Setting up Facebook

The **Facebook Connect** feature, which we have been seeing under the login form, allows users who already have a Facebook account to create an account on our site by using their Facebook login. This feature could be useful; users don't have to create new accounts with a different username and password.

In order to enable Facebook login, we need the **Facebook API Key** and **Facebook Application Secret**. These can be obtained by creating a Facebook app. We will need a Facebook account to do so. Follow these steps to set this up:

1. Go to: `http://developers.facebook.com/setup/` and log in with your Facebook login. Enter any information that you are prompted for.

2. Click on the developer dashboard.

3. The next page will ask you to import your app into the developer's page. After this you will see your **Facebook API key** and **Facebook Application Secret**. Click on **Edit settings** and complete the form. Follow the directions closely.

4. Log in to the back-end of the website—**Components | JomSocial | Configurations | Facebook Connect**. Enter the **Facebook API key** and **Facebook Application Secret**, configure the settings, and save.

5. Refresh the page, and then click on the **Facebook Connect** icon on the site. A dialog box similar to the one shown in the following screenshot will open if the settings are correct. Users can now log in to our site by using their Facebook account.

After a user logs in with their Facebook account, Jomsocial will automatically create a copy of their Facebook profile within the network. This becomes a single sign in for both Facebook and the JomSocial.

> Users will always have to use their Facebook login to log in to our site. And, whenever they use their Facebook login, it will automatically launch their account on our network.

Setting up Twitter

We will go through two Twitter setups, and of course, we need to have a Twitter account to be able to do this.

Setting up Twitter as an application for ALL of our users

When we first set up JomSocial, we indicated that the professional version is packaged with 23 applications, one of which is **My twitter updates** (this can also be downloaded from the JomSocial website—see **Addons**). Administrators of sites can make this application available for users to install and show on their profile. This application can be used to update user activities regularly, through their tweets.

The Twitter plugin was one of the apps that we enabled when we started. Let's check to see if the Twitter application is active. Go to the Joomla! back-end and carry out the following steps:

1. From the administrative back-end, click on **Components** | **JomSocial** | **Applications**. Activate the app if it still disabled. This makes the application available for our users to make it a part of their profiles. We can also choose to make it a part of all user profiles, core applications.

2. Log into the frontend and go to **Applications** | **Browse**. Locate **My twitter updates**. Add it.

3. When the dialog box opens, click on **Settings,** to complete the process.

Once this has been set up and the connection established, users' Twitter updates become a part of their profile. This may take a few minutes.

Tweets will begin to show here when a user starts tweeting. Login information can also be checked by clicking on the tool button if tweets do not display after a while.

Setting up Twitter to share information about the site

There are various Twitter modules that can be integrated with Joomla!. We downloaded JF Twitter from the Joomla! website. To set it up, follow these steps:

1. From the administrative back-end, click on **Extensions | install/uninstall**, and install the Twitter module.

2. After the installation, go to **Extensions**, choose **Modules**, and find **JF Twitter**. Enter the Twitter information, the module position, and the pages on which you want it to appear. We will set the administrator tweets to show up on the **Listings** page. Save and refresh the page. It may take a few minutes for tweets to appear on the site.

Adding other items to the HelloMe module

HelloMe is a JomSocial module designed to give quick access to certain menu items. This module can be used as a shortcut to some menu items when users drift away from the menu page. We will set it to appear on the **Listings & Review** page, after a user logs in. This is a deliberate act of positioning to create an intuitive interface so that our site users can add listings and check their messages from any page.

Access and enable the HelloMe module from the administrator back-end. We have enabled it and set the access level to **registered**. Log in from the front-end and navigate to the **Listings & Review** page.

The module has some quick access links to menu items that can be activated or deactivated through the module settings.

With a simple hack, we can add more items to the module for easy access. The file that needs to be edited can be found in the `modules` folder that is accessed through an FTP client with this path: `modules/mod_hellome/helper.php`. Before you make any hacks, make sure that you back up the file, or make a copy of it.

1. Open the `helper.php` file in a web editor such as Dreamweaver or Nvu. There are lots of lines of code—each represents an item that appears on the HelloMe module, depending on what is activated.

2. We will try to break it down. Scroll through the code to lines 111-116. This code represents the last item on the `hello_me` module: `My videos`.

3. The first part indicates that if the videos' link is enabled (`if($enablevideos) { ?>`), then it should appear with an icon:

```
<div style="background: transparent url(<?php echo JURI::
root(); ?>modules/mod_hellome/images/icons-16x16.gif) no-repeat
0 -398px; padding: 0 0 0 22px;">
```

and poing to this link:

```
<a style="line-height: 18px;" href="<?php echo CRoute::_
('index.php?option=com_community&view=videos&task=myvideos&user
id='.$myId); ?>"><?php echo JText::_('MOD_HELLOME MY VIDEOS');
?></a>
</div>
```

4. Because the features that we want to add are not a part of the original coding, we will not add the `if enabled` part. Let's duplicate the code and add it below the video code. Save and then upload the file, and preview the `hello_me` module.

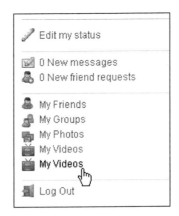

Notice that another link to **My Videos** has appeared after uploading the edited `helper.php`.

Now we know that we can add other items to the menu. Let's add a link for adding listings (**Add Listings**). To add such a link, carry out the steps below:

1. Change the address that the link should point to. Look for the code: `href="<?php echo CRoute:_ ?>`. Change the address to the new address: `index.php?newaddress` to allow users to add new listings.

2. Next, we need to provide the menu title. We need to change it from **My Videos** to **Add Listings**. Locate the text **MOD_HELLOME MY VIDEOS** and change it to **Add listings**. Save and upload document. Refresh the page and you will notice a new menu item in the module.

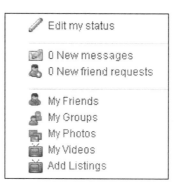

To make things really fancy, we created a new menu that is visible to registered members for easy access to add new listings. Click on the menu item and it will take you there. Users can also check their mail and log out from this menu.

Moving installed apps to above the activity stream

The JomSocial front page displays the user activity stream if this has been activated. Each user's activity stream also appears in their profile. Unlike the front page, the administrator or users do not have the option to deactivate the activity stream for user profiles. However, a simple hack can move the activity stream to below the installed applications.

Users profile pages can be edited by accessing the `profile.index.php` file, which is located in the JomSocial template folder. In the previous chapter, we duplicated the default folder and called it kifari. So, we need to look in the same folder to make any modifications to the profile main page.

1. Locate the file that you need to edit: `yourwebsite.com/components/com_community/templates/kifari/profile.index.php` and open the file in Dreamweaver or Nvu (or other HTML editor).

2. Locate the code between lines 54 and 63.

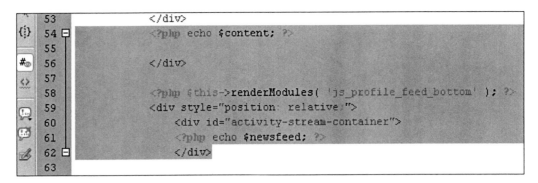

`<?php echo $content; ?>` represents the content generated through the applications.

`<?php echo $newsfeed; ?>` represents the activity stream.

3. Change to the code above to match the following code, in order to move things. Save and then upload your changes and then refresh page to see the changes. Notice that individual streams have moved.

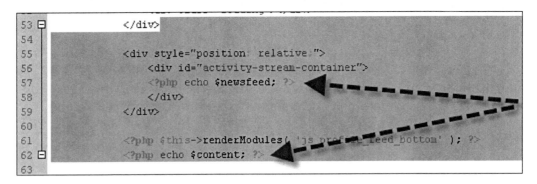

| Home | Profile | Friends | Applications | To do list | Inbox | | Logout |

Share this

jlord_text_user100

I'm getting good at this

- Member since
- Tuesday, 30 September 2008 04:01
- Last online
- less than a minute ago
- Profile views
- 6 views

My Status

Share your thoughts here...

- Edit profile
- Change profile picture
- Privacy
- Add Video

- Add applications
- Start a new group
- Invite Friends

- Write Message
- View your Inbox
- Upload photos

jlord_text_user100 & friends | jlord_text_user100

My Listings

ylrmg

☐☐☐☐☐ 0.0   ☐☐☐☐☐ 0.0

Category: Apple

Where

☐☐☐☐☐ 0.0   ☐☐☐☐☐ 5.0

Category: Other

Pandora

☐☐☐☐☐ 4.3   ☐☐☐☐☐ 5.0 (1)

Category: Other

MusicID

☐☐☐☐☐ 0.0   ☐☐☐☐☐ 4.5 (1)

Category: Apple

Reviews of Me

There are no user reviews for this listing.

[Add new review]

My Favorites

MobiVJ

☐☐☐☐☐ 0.0   ☐☐☐☐☐ 4.0 (1)

Category: Apple

Yesterday

jlord_text_user100 added new listing ylrmg in Apple. ◄— — — — Activity stream™ ✕

Latest Reviews

Where

☐☐☐☐☐ 5.0

Reviewed by jlord_text_user100

Pandora

☐☐☐☐☐ 5.0

Reviewed by jlord_text_user100

Pandora

☐☐☐☐☐ 4.3

Reviewed by d.deshdababa

About Me

Basic Information

Friends

0 friends.

Show all

Scroll To Top

Joomla! SEF

No Joomla! site is complete without SEF (Search Engine Friendly) web addresses.

1. To enable SEF, go to the Joomla! back-end, click on **Site | Global Configuration**, and change the **SEO Setting** from **No** to **Yes**.

2. Next we need to edit the `configuration.php` file in order for SEO to be effective. Locate the file with the path `rootfolder/configuration.php`. This can be edited by using a web authoring tool like Dreamweaver, Nvu, or KompoZer.

```
20      var $live_site = '';
21      var $force_ssl = '0';
22      var $offset = '0';
```

Change the `live_site` value to the site name; in our case, this is `http://www.kifari.com`, as shown in the next image. When you make this change, the title alias in Joomla! becomes very significant, so we will have to pay attention to that as the alias will be used by Joomla! to create the SEF addresses.

```
20      var $live_site = 'http://www.kifari.com';
21      var $force_ssl = '0';
22      var $offset = '0';
```

JomSocial also supports SEF (Search Engine Friendly) or SEO (Search Engine Optimization), and this is available under JomSocial configuration. We can choose between two possible settings: username/features or features/username.

By activating the SEF or SEO on our site, we will change complex URLs such as: `http://kifari.com/index.php?option=com_community&view=profile&userid=62&Itemid=2` to a simple ones like `http://www.kifari.com`.

Changing the messages

We can also customize our site's invitation messages that are sent to invitees, by editing the `en-GB.com_community.ini` file at the following path in the Joomla! root folder: `rootfolder\language\en-GB\en-GB.com_community.ini`. Edit the message around line 209:

```
Line 209: CC INVITE EMAIL MESSAGE=%1$s invites you to join %2$s
```

Other messages can also be changed in this file.

Video and photo upload sizes

It is essential to have the php.ini file created in order to take care of file uploads and memory issues. We may have to check the control panel of our hosting company and create a php.ini file for site optimization. The video and photo file upload size limits need to be specified in the php.ini file to ensure that our site runs smoothly.

To make these changes, we will have to increase the maximum file size for posting and uploading, after we have created the php.ini file. Search for the following values, and change them in the php.ini file to the desired values:

1. post_max_size = 2M
2. upload_max_filesize = 2M

If you are unsure of what you are doing, you may have to contact your hosting support for some direction on how to address this issue.

Summary

After making the changes and using some of the tips outlined in this chapter, we now have some insight into how we can customize our site and create a user friendly interface for an effective user experience that will hopefully make our site a success.

We need to keep good documentation of the changes that we have made, and have a back-up version so that we can use this to restore changes if necessary. This is essential because an upgrade of the social networking component of our site may remove some of the customizations that we have made. Unfortunately, that is the harsh reality. Hopefully, we may not have to do much when we upgrade our system.

This chapter concludes our work with JomSocial extensions. In the next chapter, we will briefly discuss other Joomla! extensions that can also be used to develop social networking sites.

9
Other Joomla! Social Networking Extensions

Throughout this book, we have worked on JomSocial, a Joomla! extension that works right out of the box with minimal customization. However, there are various other social networking and community-building Joomla! extensions. In this chapter, we discuss such extensions, which are still being actively developed and updated: Community Builder, JSocial Suite, Linksutra, CBE, Tuiyo, and Odude. These community building and social networking extensions are to be considered as alternatives to the JomSocial Joomla! social networking component. We will discuss Community Builder and JSocial Suite in some detail.

We can also install these extensions on our local host for testing, and then use the Akeebabackup Joomla! backup extension to back up the installation and migrate it to a remote host.

Community Builder

Community Builder is one of the oldest Joomla! social networking extensions. It has over 150 free or commercial plugins. The plugins provide a lot of flexibility in the development of a Community Builder-driven social networking platform. They allow us to integrate a lot of features into a social network developed using the Joomla! Community Builder extension. Because Community Builder is one of the oldest Joomla! extensions, it is important to check and review the plugins that can be installed as add-ons before we install them. The Joomla! core engine has changed so much that some developers of extensions have not been able to keep up with the pace of development.

To install Community Builder, we will have to register on its official website at http://www.joomlapolis.com for a free account. However, not all Community Builder plugins are free; there are both commercial modules and plugins, listed on the Joomla! official website. In this chapter, we identify a few free plugins that can be used to develop a social network similar to the one that we built with JomSocial.

Visit http://www.joomlapolis.com to register, and then download a copy of the Community Builder component for installation. By now, we are familiar with the installation of Joomla! Extensions, so we will go ahead and install Community Builder. The Community Builder installation package comes with four zip files:

- The com_comprofiler component is the core Community Builder component
- mod_cblogin (a Community Builder-specific login module)
- mod_comprofilerModerator (notifies the moderator of pending actions)
- mod_comprofilerOnline (who's online in Community Builder)

Community Builder (CB) does not work with the default Joomla! login module, so the first thing that we have to do after the installation of Community Builder is to disable the existing Joomla! login module and enable the mod_cblogin and mod_comprofilerOnline modules for users.

After installation, we will configure CB by accessing its back-end through **Components | Community Builder**. It is absolutely essential to publish or enable the modules (especially the mod_comprofiler module) in order to be able to get access to our profile when we log in from the front-end. Take a look at the profile interface after installation. Do so by logging in at the front-end and clicking on your username. This opens the Profile interface of CB, as shown in the following screenshot:

Unlike JomSocial, CB comes with only three modules. This gives us the flexibility to add on any features that we want as a part of our social network. However, it will require some research into Joomla! plugins that are built specifically for integrations with CB, or any Joomla! plugin that is compatible with CB. Good places to start are the CB official website and the extensions page on the Joomla! official website.

Also, in contrast with JomSocial, Community Builder has an integral option for choosing different avatars available within the CB installation; by just clicking on the edit button; we can also upload an avatar.

CB uses a tab system to display its tool menu when a user logs in. To have various tools enabled for our users, we need to install extensions (modules, plugins, and components needed for enabling specific tools or applications). CB-compatible extensions, when installed and enabled, appear as a part of the tools or applications that are available to our users; they appear as a part of the tab system.

If we wanted to have similar features to the app reviews websites with our Community Builder, we would carry out the activities described in the following section:

Making connections and integrating with others

Similar to most social networking systems like Facebook, it is always easy to determine who is part of the CB network. If the "Who's Online" module is published, we can see who is online and try to interact with them. We can also see who's on the site as people participate in activities.

There are some modules, such as **cb random users**, that allows an administrator to feature users on the site. This information can be published in a module position to showcase different users on the site, each time that page is refreshed.

Directory/Review feature

SOBI2 (available at: `http://joomla.sigsiu.net/`) also integrates seamlessly into CB. We can use some of the steps laid out in *Chapter 5, Creating Content and Sharing Activities* to integrate SOBI into CB. Although this component is used mainly as a directory system, it is also fully extensible by using compatible modules and plugins to add features to its core functions and then integrate with other extensions in a Joomla! installation.

Messaging feature

UddeIM is a messaging extension (component, modules, and plugins) that can be used to add a messaging tool or application to CB.

Following are the steps to install UddeIM:

1. Download the package from `http://www.slabihoud.de/software/id4001.htm` (we can also find information at `extensions.joomla.org`).

2. The package downloaded comes with the component (`com_uddeim`); modules (`mode_uddeim`, `mod_uddeim_mailbox`, `mod_uddeim_statistics`) and plugins (`cb_plug_pms_uddeim`, `cb_plug_pms_uddeim_inbox`, `plug_uddeim_pms_contentlink`, `cb_plug_pms_uddeim_blocking`). Any plugin, with CB identification is a plugin that integrates with Community Builder.

3. Use the default Joomla! extension installation process in order to install the components and modules. The UddeIM component can be configured (**Components | UddeIM**). We can also enable the modules and place them in preferred module positions.

4. Community Builder plugins need to be installed through the Community Builder plugin installation system, **Components | Community builder | Plugin Management** and not the Joomla! extension installation:

5. After we log in, notice the UddeIM Mailbox module. This gives us access to the messaging component. Click on **Inbox** to see if we have any mail; there is none of course. Click on **Compose** to send an e-mail to someone that you are connected with. Let's send an e-mail to the admin.

6. Publish the CB plugins, and let us figure out how it works.

16	☐	PMS uddeIM	✓	✗	▲	▼	99	Public	user	pms.uddeim
17	☐	PMS uddeIM Inbox	✓	✗	▲	▼	99	Public	user	pms.showinbox
18	☐	uddeIM Blocking Plugin	✓	✗	▲	▼	99	Public	user	blocking.uddeim
19	☐	uddeIM Profilelink	✓	✗	▲		99	Public	user	pms.uddeim.profilelink

Display # 20 ⌄   << Start < Prev 1 Next > End >>   **Results 1 - 19 of total 19**

Install New Plugin

Upload Package File

Package File: [_____] Browse... Upload File & Install

7. Once the modules and plugins are enabled, we can view them from the front-end.

The **UddeIM Mailbox** module allows us to access our mailbox from the module. When we click on the message, we will be able to access our mailbox and start sending out messages.

Any messages that we send (that we request a copy of) and messages that are sent to us can be accessed here. UddeIM has some fascinating features. For instance, we can recall messages and keep deleted files in the trash can, just like the recycling bin of a computer.

Changing the tab names

Notice that after we installed the messaging system, the tab associated with it had the name **_UE_TABINBOX**. No one will know what **_UE_TABINBOX** is. The tabs can be renamed by going to **Components | Community Builder | Tab Management**. Click on the name of a tab and edit it.

| 15 | | Blocking | The Blocking Tab | tab | uddeIM Blocking Plugin | ✓ | Everybody | tabmain | ▲ | ▼ | 101 | 24 |
| 16 | | _UE_TABINBOX | | tab | PMS uddeIM Inbox | ✓ | Everybody | tabmain | ▲ | | 102 | 25 |

Adding multimedia

Adding multimedia is at the core of every social network. Users should be able to show images and videos on their profile, and be able to share such content with others. Like any other extension, we will have to identify a CB-compatible extension in order to make such tools available to users.

A gallery tool that can be integrated with CB is JoomGallery, which has a plugin for CB. Video can also be added by installing the **CB Video Player**.

Community Builder groups and communities

In order to facilitate group activities in the Community Builder online network environment, we need to install another component called GroupJive.

GroupJive is one of the earliest social networking tools for creating communities on a Joomla! site. At the time of its release, most of the Joomla! social networking tools focused mainly on one-to-one communications and interaction. GroupJive facilitated the setting up of communities within a Joomla! site. Over time, the project became dormant, and in May 2009 Joomlapolis, the creators of Community Builder, took over the project. GroupJive requires Community Builder or Community Builder Enhanced to work in the Joomla! environment.

The latest stable version of GroupJive was released as we were writing this book (April 30, 2010), thus providing us with the opportunity to share and showcase its latest features. Download GroupJive from the `joomlapolis.com` website (you will need to log in first). The file downloaded contains two files: `com_groupjive_1.8.zip` (the GJ component package) and `plug_cbgroupjive.zip` (the GJ CB Plugin package).

Install the component through the Joomla! extension installer, and the plugin through the Community Builder Plugin Management installer, and enable it. We can also create a direct link to GroupJive to enable direct access to it. This is where users will create groups and interact. Like any other Joomla! component, we need to configure and check the settings, link it from the main menu, and interact.

Groups

WELCOME TO GROUPS
You can visit groups, join groups or create your own.

Search for a group... [Search]
Create your OWN Group!

Categories of Community Groups

Droid (0)

iPhones (1)

[Reset Settings]   Scroll To Top

The admin interface of the group is also very simple.

Group Activities   **Manager**

foursquare

jlord_test_user100

- Group type: Open to all
- Founded: 06.05.2010
- Group Members: 1
- Manager: jlord_test_user100

Managers Tasks

- Group Members
- Group Bulletins
- Return to Group

- Invite People (+)
- Email Group Manager

- MANAGE *pending users*
- EDIT *group settings*
- EMAIL *all in group*
- TRANSFER *to new owner*
- DELETE ~~this group~~

New Members   **Latest bulletin**

There are no messages in group bulletin

jlord_test_user100

Users need to be logged in to create or participate in group activities. If a user creates or joins a group, that group becomes a part of their profile, and if the group plugin is activated, users can interact with their groups directly from their profile.

| Contact Info | Additional Info | Mailbox | Groups | | | | |

Group▼▲	Category▼▲	Creator▼▲	Type▼▲	Members	Joined▼▲
foursquare	iPhones	jlord_test_user 100	Open	1	05/06/2010

Integrating Twitter and Facebook

We can integrate existing social networks like Facebook and Twitter into Community Builder. In May 2010, Joomlapolis released the first stable CB Facebook and CB Twitter Connect authentication plugins. Those two plugins enable users to connect to a CB-driven social network by using their Twitter and Facebook accounts, similar to what we did with JomSocial. One needs to be a CB documentation subscriber in order to gain access to these tools.

For those who do not want to pay to subscribe, the Twitter for Community Builder or Twitter tab plugins (available from the Joomla! extensions website) are free options that enable users to display their tweets on their profile.

Here is an example of how the Twitter tab plugin (http://www.1st-movers.com/) appears under the user profile of CB. Users simply need to click on **Activate your twitter account**, enter their user information, and then user tweets will appear here.

Another option for displaying social networks is to use the CB social networks plugin (http://www.juntehispano.com), which enables us to display links to about 10 of our networks at the same time. All we need to do is to add our social network username, and a link will be shown on our profile.

The same website also has an RSS feeds feature, for adding RSS feeds, called Multifeed. This allows users to add RSS feeds to their profiles.

Changing the layout (tips and tricks)

Throughout our brief overview of Community Builder, all of the tools or applications appeared in tabs. The administrator can change the positions of various features in order to change the look of the site's user panel. Community Builder has many CB-specific positions that can be used to change the overall look of the profile page, similar to the JomSocial profile page positions that we saw in *Chapter 8, Tips and Tricks*.

The changes can be made from the back-end by going to **Components | Community Builder (CB) | Tab management**. Notice that different features are in different positions:

#	□	Title	Description	Display	Plugin	Published	Access	Position	Re-Order	⚒	Tabid
1	□	Menu		html	CB Menu	✓	Everybody	head	▼	-10	17
2	□	Connection Paths		html	CB Connections	✓	Everybody	head	▲ ▼	-9	18
3	□	User Profile Page Title		html	CB Core	✓	Everybody	head	▲	-8	19
4	□	Portrait		html	CB Core	✓	Everybody	middle		-7	20
5	□	User Status		html	CB Menu	✓	Everybody	right	▼	-6	21
6	□	Quick Message		html	Private Message System	✗	Everybody	right	▲ ▼	-5	22
7	□	Quick Message		html	PMS uddeIM	✓	Everybody	right	▼	100	23
8	□	_UE_PMSLINK		html	uddeIM Profilelink	✓	Everybody	right	▲	103	26
9	□	Contact Info		tab	CB Core	✓	Everybody	tabmain	▼	-4	11
10	□	Articles		tab	Content Author	✗	Everybody	tabmain	▲ ▼	-3	12
11	□	Forum		tab	Forum Integration	✗	Everybody	tabmain	▲ ▼	-2	13
12	□	Blog		tab	Mamiblog Blog	✗	Everybody	tabmain	▲ ▼	-1	14
13	□	Connections		tab	CB Connections	✗	Everybody	tabmain	▲ ▼	99	15

The tab system (tabmain) is the default for adding features. Each feature added automatically becomes a tab.

But what if we do not want everything in a tab? How do we do that? Community Builder offers over 90 profile positions to choose from. Let's make a few changes to the mailbox tab.

1. Go to **Components | Community Builder (CB) | Tab management**.
2. Click on mailbox (remember, the one that we renamed).
3. Change the position and display time, then save and preview.

Position:	Main area (below left/middle/right) ⌄	Position on profile and ordering on registration.
Display type:	Rounded div with title ⌄	In which way the content of this tab will be displayed on the profile.

4. Notice that the mailbox is no longer in a tab and occupies its own position. Explore the other positions and display type to determine what best meets your needs..

In order to add applications or tools for interactivity on a CB-driven social network, it is always good to first check if a component, module, or plugin exists for the feature that we want to add. We will have to determine whether it is commercial or free and how users are going to interact with or use the tools. For instance, if we intend to offer Google advertisements, we can locate an extension that allows for the integration of Google ads within the CB social network.

Our discussion of the CB Joomla! extension for social networking is not complete in terms of what can be achieved with setting up a social network using CB. We have simply demonstrated the potential of this Joomla! extension. A complete book can be written on this component alone. This discussion is intended to be an insightful introduction to the subject pointing out the potential of the CB component as a social networking tool. There are over 150 CB-specific plugins that can be found at http://extensions.joomla.org/—**Categories | Extension Specific | Community builder extensions**.

> Note that for a standalone component to be integrated with Community Builder, we need to have a CB plugin. What we suggest is that you first determine if plugins are available for a component that you intend to use. The Joomla! website has nicely categorized plugins for Community Builder.

In summary, Community Builder also provides a lot of tools and flexibility for building social networks. It may take a bit more time to research and find all of the tools necessary to build an interactive site. While some documentation is available, one needs to have a paid subscription to the Community Builder Documentation Membership to get access to some of the CB plugins and more comprehensive documentation.

JSocialSuite

JSocialSuite (http://www.jsocialsuite.com) is another social networking component for Joomla!. It is commercial, with a GPL license, and was released in April 2010 as we were writing this book. It comes with three subscription options (basic, premier, and developer). We created an account on the JSocialSuite website in order to access the demo for a better understanding of the features of this component (click on the **Community** link after creating and activating your account).

1. This component provides users with the option to choose individualized templates. As we were completing the registration process, we had the option to choose a template. Instead of all users having a uniform look, jSocialSuite allows users to choose a template from a set of templates made available to users, as shown in the following screenshot:

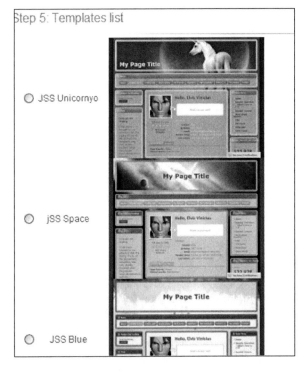

2. Users can manage their applications after selecting a template. Users can also add applications.

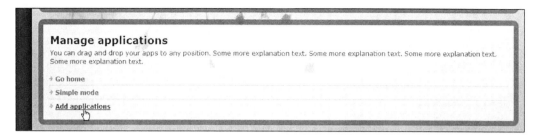

The process for adding applications it quite simple; it even facilitates the duplication of apps. By clicking on **Simple mode**, users are able to rearrange the apps' positions, and customize user profile.

3. A click on **Home** sends users to their main profile.

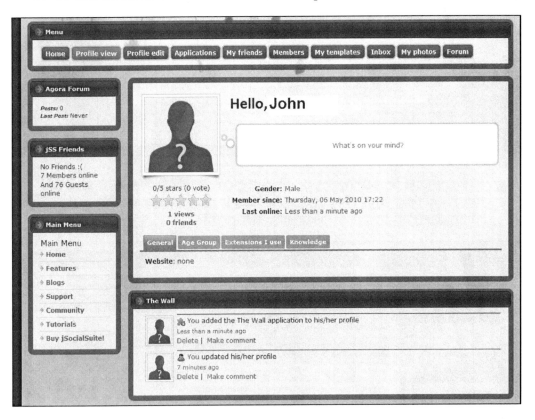

4. The features are easily accessible from the top menu, making it easy for users to interact. The features available on the demo site are: **User Selectable Templates, Built-in Photo Gallery, Agora Forum, Integration, The Wall Status Features, Commenting System, Personal Announcements, VitalPM Advanced Messaging, Full Function Twitter App, User Positionable Apps, Blog/RSS Feed Reader, Community Visibility/Privacy Settings,** and **Configurable Friends App.**

This is a Joomla! social networking component to look out for. Just like JomSocial, it appears to be a ready pre-packaged component. As a new component, there are very few extensions developed to integrate this component into other extensions.

Other social networking components

Joomla! has other social networking components that we identified. In this section, we discuss briefly a few of these components that appear to be updated regularly. Whereas some components take minimal time for installation and use, others may require more time, patience, and customization to get them running with the required user interface. CBE, Linksutra, Odude, and Joomunity are additional Joomla! social networking extensions that could be considered as possible candidates for social networking on the Joomla! site.

CBE for Joomla!

CBE is an enhanced version of the Community Builder component (`http://www.joomla-cbe.de/`). The demo on the official website indicates that is has a lot of features in common with Community Builder. It was initially developed in German, and there may be some progress towards translating it into English.

Linksutra social networking

Linksutra (`http://linksutra.com/index.php`) offers a simple Joomla! social networking component. It has a scrapbook, albums, and demands and offers features. The demands and offers features can be used for online bidding or e-commerce. It allows users to bid or make offers on business transactions. A demo can be found at `http://demo.linksutra.com/index.php`.

Odude Profile

Odude Profile is a Joomla! social networking component that can be used primarily for dating sites. A live demo can be seen at `http://lovelynepal.com/portal/member.html`. Visit Odude at `http://www.odude.com/home/`.

Tuiyo (aka Joomunity)

Tuiyo, formerly called Joomunity, has undergone some development to facilitate smooth integration with Joomla!. It allows users to change their templates, provides multiple language support, widgets for other social networks, feeds, and group activities. More information on this extension can be found at `http://apps.tuiyo.co.uk/`.

Summary

Joomla! has encouraged the development of various social networking components to facilitate diverse social networking platforms for diverse online activities and rich user experiences. Each extension or component could be the subject of a book.

We hope this book offered you an insightful understanding of the options available for developing a social networking site with Joomla!. As we have learned, JomSocial is an excellent candidate for setting up a Joomla! social networking site, but there exist other formidable candidates for building social networks on the same Joomla! platform. Even though our discussion was largely based on JomSocial, there is no doubt that we can explore building a Joomla!-driven social networking site by using any of the other Joomla! extensions.

Index

Thank you for buying
Joomla! Social Networking with JomSocial

About Packt Publishing

Packt, pronounced 'packed', published its first book "*Mastering phpMyAdmin for Effective MySQL Management*" in April 2004 and subsequently continued to specialize in publishing highly focused books on specific technologies and solutions.

Our books and publications share the experiences of your fellow IT professionals in adapting and customizing today's systems, applications, and frameworks. Our solution based books give you the knowledge and power to customize the software and technologies you're using to get the job done. Packt books are more specific and less general than the IT books you have seen in the past. Our unique business model allows us to bring you more focused information, giving you more of what you need to know, and less of what you don't.

Packt is a modern, yet unique publishing company, which focuses on producing quality, cutting-edge books for communities of developers, administrators, and newbies alike. For more information, please visit our website: www.packtpub.com.

About Packt Open Source

In 2010, Packt launched two new brands, Packt Open Source and Packt Enterprise, in order to continue its focus on specialization. This book is part of the Packt Open Source brand, home to books published on software built around Open Source licences, and offering information to anybody from advanced developers to budding web designers. The Open Source brand also runs Packt's Open Source Royalty Scheme, by which Packt gives a royalty to each Open Source project about whose software a book is sold.

Writing for Packt

We welcome all inquiries from people who are interested in authoring. Book proposals should be sent to author@packtpub.com. If your book idea is still at an early stage and you would like to discuss it first before writing a formal book proposal, contact us; one of our commissioning editors will get in touch with you.

We're not just looking for published authors; if you have strong technical skills but no writing experience, our experienced editors can help you develop a writing career, or simply get some additional reward for your expertise.

[PACKT] open source ✳
PUBLISHING   community experience distilled

Joomla! Template Design

ISBN: 978-1-847191-44-1   Paperback: 232 pages

A complete guide for web designers to all aspects of designing unique website templates for the free Joomla! 1.0.8 PHP Content Management System

1. Create Joomla! Templates for your sites

2. Debug, validate, and package your templates

3. Tips for tweaking existing templates

Joomla! 1.5: Beginner's Guide

ISBN: 978-1-847199-90-4   Paperback: 380 pages

Build and maintain impressive user-friendly web sites the fast and easy way with Joomla! 1.5

1. Create a web site that meets real-life requirements by following the creation of an example site with the help of easy-to-follow steps and ample screenshots

2. Practice all the Joomla! skills from organizing your content to completely changing the site's looks and feel

3. Go beyond a typical Joomla! site to make the site meet your specific needs

4. Get to grips with inspiring examples and best practices and implement them to enhance your Joomla! site

Please check **www.PacktPub.com** for information on our titles

LaVergne, TN USA
30 August 2010
195185LV00003B/24/P